The Great American BASEBALL SCRAPBOOK

THE Gr
Amer
BASE
SCRAP

A Rutledge Book   Random House

eat
ican
BALL
BOOK

by A. D. Suehsdorf
Pat Quinn, Consultant

For Betty, teammate

memorabilia from:
Sports Collectors Store
Charles ("Buck") Barker
Ed Budnick
Dick Dobbins
Barry Halper
Donald Steinbach

Editorial	Art Direction
Fred R. Sammis	Allan Mogel
John Sammis	*Production*
Jeremy Friedlander	Lori Stein
Beverlee Galli	
Jay Hyams	
Susan Lurie	

Copyright © 1978 by Rutledge Books, Inc. All rights reserved. No part of this book may be reproduced or transmitted in any form or by any means, electronic or mechanical, including photocopying, recording or by any information storage and retrieval system, without permission in writing from the Publisher.

Library of Congress Cataloging in Publication Data

Suehsdorf, A. D.
  The great American baseball scrapbook.

  "A Rutledge book."
  1. Baseball—Miscellanea. 2. Baseball—History.
I. Title.
GV867.3.S93   796.357'09   78-5021
ISBN: 0-394-50253-1

Random House, Inc.
201 East 50th Street
New York, NY 10022
First Edition 1978
Printed in the United States of America

Editor's Note

Scrapbooks are random, personal, and always incomplete. They are reminders of good times past, tokens of people, events, and warm feeling that memory has decided to preserve. A good scrapbook puts distance between you and its contents. It cannot concern time too raw or recent. It prefers time that has mellowed, whose edges have begun to curl. For such reasons, this good scrapbook stops in 1969.

Chapter 1

THE PASTIME GOES PRO

1876~1900

These were the morning years of professional baseball in America. The National League was founded as they began (and completed its first, seventy-game season as the Hayes-Tilden presidential election approached). The American League was about to begin its first season as they ended. Between were years of discovery. Baseball techniques and strategies were being explored and refined. Much baseball action now regarded as routine was happening for the first time.

The period seems quaint and far away; few people today have memories of even its latest date. Yet in spirit and in fact it is closer to us than we are accustomed to think. The century since 1876 can be comfortably spanned by the careers of only five players, and a contemporary fan enabled to reverse time and attend a game in, say, 1884, might be surprised to recognize more similarities with 1970s baseball than differences from it.

These factors—the continuity of player generations and the speed with which the game established its basic form—are at the heart of baseball's strong and persistent appeal. These plus the fact that, more than in any other sport, what goes on can be measured statistically. Uniforms change, stadiums change, and styles of play undergo subtle alterations, but the dimensions of the diamond appear to have been perfectly calculated to maximize excitement and uncertainty in the historic processes of scoring runs. Whatever the situation, the speed of pitched and batted balls and the speed of fielders' throws are exquisitely coordinated with the speed of baserunners. Such rhythms are constants in players' performances and in observers' expectations, and baseball's volumes of statistics are simply expressions of how successfully the traditional maneuvers of the game have been executed.

Five players to span a century: Who are they? To begin with, Adrian Constantine ("Cap") Anson, who played first base for the Chicago White Stockings (later the Colts, then the Cubs) from 1876 to 1897 and averaged .333 for those twenty-two years. Cap's final year—he was deemed virtually irreplaceable and his Colts became the Orphans the season after his departure—saw the debut with Louisville of a burly young shortstop named Hans Wagner. (The Grays' other prize rookie that year was Rube Waddell!) Marvelous Hans, the choice of many National League partisans as the finest player of all time, was active through 1917, when he was forty-three and had had three seasons in which to observe the hard-eyed, implacable Rogers Hornsby, already on his way, at twenty-one, toward a lifetime average of .358, second only to Ty Cobb's incredible .367. Hornsby bowed out in 1937, as Bob Feller began to blossom at Cleveland. And "Rapid Robert" was still throwing in 1954, when Hank Aaron came up with the Milwaukee Braves.

Many such combinations are possible, of course: Dan Brouthers, Cobb, Paul Waner, Warren Spahn, and Brooks Robinson, for instance, cover almost the same period. Every career naturally overlaps others, but the point of the exercise is to demonstrate how closely knit the baseball fabric really is, how the links between lives can bind a century together.

The Hornsby of 1926, the Cardinal manager who summoned the hungover Grover Cleveland Alexander from the bullpen to fan Tony Lazzeri and go on to win the Series, had seen the great Wagner of a past era, would glimpse the potential of Feller (eight years old in 1926), but would not

PHILLIPS, 1st Base, BROOKLYN

BROUTHERS, 1st Base, DETROIT

live to see Tom Seaver, Rod Carew, or Pete Rose. Alex in 1926 still had 46 games to win to get his 373, but his past had a longer reach than his future: he went back to 1911, when Cy Young still was in the National League. On the other hand, Waite Hoyt, the Yankees' losing pitcher in that seventh game, would play on to 1938 in the company of such as Al Simmons, Luke Appling, and Mel Ott—long enough to see the young Joe DiMaggio, not quite long enough to see either Ted Williams or Stan Musial.

What, in fact, was baseball—or Base Ball, as it was called for many years—like in 1884?

Fundamentally, it was the game played today, but with important modifications still to come. Batters were retired on three strikes (although fouls were not yet counted), and catchers, just learning how to position themselves under the bat, had to grab the third one on the fly for it to be an out. Walks were another matter. At one time nine balls rated a walk. In other seasons it was eight, seven, six. Not until 1889 was agreement reached, once and for all, on four.

The pitcher's box was literally that: a four-by-six-foot rectangle marked on the ground fifty feet from home plate. The shorter flight path gave the pitchers a significant advantage, particularly since the various unenforceable rules requiring them to throw underhand had just been abolished. Since their repertoire already included the curve, sinker (drop), screwball (in-curve), and change-up, the new freedom to utilize the catapult action of the overhand fastball made pitchers imposing indeed and undoubtedly contributed to their astonishing ability to win forty-five and fifty games a season. Of course, pitchers still threw from level ground; the mound was not yet in use. So, however swift the reflexes needed to put bat to ball from fifty feet, the best hitters—Anson, Brouthers, and Mike ("King") Kelly—evidently had no difficulty achieving .350 averages.

Probably the biggest difference between then and now was in the mobility of the players. They were rather more sedate, inclined to anchor themselves to their bases, and so there was less movement to the overall action than there is now. Still, the game was far from static. Infielders were learning to back up bases and to play shallow or deep, depending on the game situation. The hit-and-run play had been devised. The strategic bunt was known, though scorned by many as a sissy hit. The art of stealing was practiced and appreciated, especially the flourish of the slide, for which sliding pads already were in use.

There was an appalling number of errors afield: 3,950 for the eight teams of the National League, or an average of 8.83 per game. The American Association and Union Association, a third major league that lasted only through the season of 1884, were even worse. Among the National Leaguers, Boston (the Beaneaters, as they were then known) was least prone to err: 3.46 per game. Anson's White Stockings, a prominent team having an off year, erred most profoundly: 5.3 per game.

Whatever its eccentricities, the game pleased the "cranks" or, as they began to be known in 1884, the "fans," an abbreviation of "fanatics" attributed to Chris Von der Ahe, the bumptious owner of the St. Louis Browns, the premier team of the American Association. Fanaticism was not too strong a word for the enthusiasm of baseball's devotees. Post-Civil War America, particularly urban America, was ready for sport and recreation. The United States was becoming the foremost industrial nation of the world, and rural Americans and European immigrants were pouring into the growing cities for jobs, high wages, and the mass entertainments that the cities offered. In the quarter century to 1900, America discovered the pleasure and excitement of its first big stakes races for horses, auto races, college football, golf, tennis, polo, and ice hockey, and had been gripped by an absolute craze for bicycling. Baseball not only took its place among these diversions; it became paramount, a sport for everyone.

By 1884, the National League was in its ninth season and professional ball had been played, first on an exhibition, roadshow basis, then with organized clubs and seasonal schedules, for some fifteen years. Crowds numbering thousands came to see the pros play. Photographs and engravings show them filling the double-decker wooden stands and overflowing onto the field along both foul lines and on the outfield perimeter. A number of foul pops behind first and third that would be routine outs today probably were not caught in those more informal times, and many a long fly must have fallen into the crowd and become a ground-rule double. Where there was no outfield fence, some spectators arrived with horse and buggy. They set the brake, eased the reins, and watched the game from their perch while Dobbin munched the center field grass. General admission was fifty cents. Tickets did not include rain checks, but would in a few more years. Ladies Day already was an institution. Some smart jasper had figured out that two games attracted crowds better than one. And in a little town in Pennsylvania in 1883 what seems to have been the first night game was played under lights. The doubleheader soon found its way into the schedule, but major league night games would be a long time coming.

Cranks behind home plate—a twelve-inch square—were protected by a stretch of chicken-wire mesh. Players sat on a bench within chatting distance; dugouts were in the offing. The Cincinnati club wore identifying numbers as early as 1883, but the idea did not catch on. Games were played in the late afternoon and everyone expected to be home for supper by six o'clock. We are used to hearing that old-time games were run off with dispatch, and, relatively, they were. But almost from the outset newspaper stories and editorials grumped that too many exceeded two hours because of dawdling on the field.

The White Stockings were the dominant team, winning five pennants between 1880 and 1886. Aside from Anson they had the ebullient King Kelly, a hard-hitting outfielder and crowd pleaser about whom the song, "Slide, Kelly, Slide" was written, and Ned Williamson, the third baseman, whose twenty-seven home runs in 1884 was the major league record until Babe Ruth came along. They also had a second-string outfielder named Billy Sunday, who won greater renown as an evangelist on the sawdust trail.

In 1884, however, the Providence Grays ran off with the flag, or "gonfalon," as sportswriters would say as they got into the swing of reporting this flamboyant game. Sixty of the Grays' eighty-four victories were contributed by "Old Hoss" Radbourn, one of the legendary figures of the game.

STRAUSS, BATTER, MILWAUKIE.

Above: *Utility man Joe Strauss played for several teams. He stands in box, preparing to swing thick bat over one-foot-square plate.* Opposite: *Cigarette cards often used same pose for many players, altering uniforms but not faces, as with barehanded first basemen John Morrill of Boston,* top, *Dan Brouthers of Detroit,* bottom, *c. 1886. Note narrow base path.*

9

Hoss, an unimposing man of middle size, had a prodigious year: a winning percentage of .833, seventy-three complete games, 678⅔ innings pitched, 441 strikeouts, and a 1.38 ERA.

As impressive a team as any was the St. Louis Browns, who won the American Association pennant four years in a row, beginning in 1885. Their player-manager was Charlie Comiskey, "the Old Roman," as he was called in tribute to his bold profile, who later became owner of the White Sox. He was never the hitter Anson was, but he was good enough and he handled his team well. Arlie Latham played a lively third base, and Tip O'Neill, a stout hitter, became a sensational one in 1887, when he achieved the tremendous average of .435. He was helped by the fact that, for that year only, walks were scored as base hits.

As can be seen from the names in early lineups, baseball was played predominantly by Irish and Germans, nationalities already well assimilated into the American population and into the urban centers where baseball made its living. Italian immigrants were arriving by the thousands, but they would not enter the game for a generation. There were supposed to be about twenty blacks playing professional ball in organized leagues, though none in the National League. No effort was made to disguise them as Indians or Cubans. They were blacks; where there was no objection they played, and where there was they didn't. They lived in the half world that always has been their lot. Baseball treated them no differently and no better than did the rest of white America. Club owners did not publicly endorse discrimination, but generally they avoided or ignored black players, so that in the end discrimination was practiced.

Moses Fleetwood Walker, an Oberlin graduate, caught for Toledo (AA) one season, and George Stovy pitched well enough for Newark, then in the Eastern League, to be considered a possiblity for New York's Gothams (soon to be Giants). Unfortunately, the move was blocked by Cap Anson, who, baseball skills aside, was a violent and active racist. He raised a rumpus over Walker, too, threatening not to play an exhibition with Toledo if Fleet were in the lineup. To its credit, Toledo told Anson to cancel and be damned, and Cap backed down. It was not the first or only time prejudice appeared on the field, however, and eventually the point of view Anson represented prevailed. By the late 1880s blacks had disappeared from white baseball.

In other respects the game improved. Lineups had to be announced before the game started, to keep heavy hitters from leaping off the bench with men on base and declaring themselves next up. Coaches were restricted to first- and third-base boxes, to keep them from running up and down the baselines, howling abuse at enemy pitchers and catchers. The plate was now made of whitened rubber. First and third bases were fixed inside the foul lines, entirely in fair territory. Batters were learning to place hits. Umpires had ball-and-strike indicators. Rudimentary chest protectors were being tried by catchers. Some left-handers still were catching or playing the infield, and adroitly, despite the extra step necessary for most throws.

Turnstiles counted the crowds, and ballplayers, by contract, could be pressed into service as ticket-takers. Players also had to furnish their own uniforms and pay for cleaning and repair. For one marvelous season (1882) it was decided to color-code the uniforms. Pitchers wore light blue ones, catchers scarlet, and so forth. Teams were supposed to be differentiated by the color and design of their hose. "Clown costumes" the players called them.

All these developments and advances bore fruit in the 1890s, when the Baltimore Orioles exploited every element of technique and play to dominate the National League as the most brilliant team anyone had ever seen. The Baltimore story is a familiar one, yet deserves retelling.

Like the Brooklyn Dodgers of a later epoch, the Orioles spent years in the wilderness until the right players and an inspirational manager came together. Originally an American Association team, the Orioles transferred to the National League in 1892 to finish twelfth in a twelve-team league. Ned Hanlon, a fiery ex-outfielder (Detroit and Pittsburgh), was the newly appointed manager. He had three players around whom to build: Wilbert Robinson, a tough, mustachioed catcher; a bantam utility man named John McGraw, barely out of the Three-I league; and Sadie McMahon, a solid, dependable pitcher. In a later metamorphosis, Robinson would be seen as the clownish, fat manager of the Brooklyn Robins in their seasons of futility, though no one could ever take away from him his grand feat of seven hits in a nine-inning game. As for McGraw, the years would change his outline but the gamecock stayed alive within him.

OLD JUDGE CIGARETTES

Outfielder Jim Fogarty demonstrates art of the slide for studio photographer in late 1880s.

Hanlon moved the team up to eighth in 1893. McGraw became the regular shortstop. Heinie Reitz came aboard to play second. Joe Kelley, a genuinely strong hitter, took over center field. By 1894, the transformation was complete. The opening-day lineup contained six future Hall-of-Famers: Robinson, McGraw (now at third), and Kelley, plus Dan Brouthers, an ex-Tiger teammate of Hanlon's at first, Hughie Jennings, short, and "Wee Willie" Keeler, right field. Reitz was at second, Steve Brodie in the outfield. Brouthers, at thirty-six, was the only veteran. Robinson was twenty-nine, the others twenty-six or under.

They tore the league apart, winning twenty-four of their last twenty-five games to take the pennant. Sadie McMahon was 25-8, but pitching really never was the Orioles' forte. Hitting was, plus, as someone has said, "hostility, imagination, speed, and piracy."

Every man in the lineup hit over .300, from Reitz's .306 to Kelley's mighty .391. And on the bases or in the field every man was a bearcat. They bunted. They played hit-and-run to perfection. They took advantage of their hard-packed infield by hitting down on the ball—the Baltimore chop—so that it would bounce high and come down too slowly to make a play at first. On defense they backed up bases, cut off throws from the outfield, and had pitchers hustling to the bag on grounders to the first baseman.

They used every trick, every wile. They tilted the baselines so that their bunts always rolled fair. They soaped the dirt around the pitcher's mound (a new addition to the topography of the playing field) so that the enemy hurler would get slippery fingers when he tried to dry his hands. They deadened balls by icing them and slipped them into the game when the opposition was at bat. They bullied the foe, they harassed and browbeat umpires, and they won three straight pennants and finished second twice before the end of the century.

LOW BALL

Buy of the Prov. Furniture Co.

This is not to say that they were successful because they were rowdy. They were more talented than that. Their swagger was meant to be intimidating and give them an edge. It was and it did.

Actually, "rowdyism" was a serious problem in the National League. Baltimore led the pack, but it was not alone. The Beaneaters and Cleveland's Spiders could play as roughly as anyone—flashing spikes, beanballs, surreptitious tripping of baserunners outside the umpire's field of vision. Everyone deplored the other fellow's roughness but did nothing to curb his own. Violence would plague the game until there was more than one umpire to control the action and until the owners were willing to empower the league president to deal forcefully with offenders.

Step by step the game advanced. The pitching distance was lengthened to its current sixty and one-half feet in 1893. The final inches were a surveyor's error. He read the zero inches of 60'0" as a 6 and pinned an immutable dimension on the game. The infield-fly rule was put into effect. Home plate became the five-sided form that fits into the apex of the first and third baselines.

More managers were confining themselves to the bench. Squads had increased as substitution rules were eased, so managers had more players to direct and more options to exercise at strategic points in the game. Catchers, because the entire field of play was spread before them, were becoming field leaders and calling specific pitches with finger signals.

Aside from Wilbert Robinson's seven hits, three other individual

Lefty in Pete Rose crouch, opposite, decorates 1883 program. "Low Ball" is what he has asked pitcher to throw him. (You could do that then.) Unprotected catcher stands out of foul-tip range. Wooden stands and top-hatted cranks are typical of times. Above: Allen & Ginter tobacco canister and handsome cards from series of c. 1887. From left are Tim Keefe, King Kelly, Monte Ward, John Clarkson, Cap Anson, and Charlie Comiskey.

records of note were established. Bobby Lowe, the Beaneaters' fine second baseman, hit four home runs in a nine-inning game in 1894. In fact he got them in three innings: two in the third, one in the fifth, the last in the sixth. Always an astonishing feat, it was all the more so for being the first time. The crowd exploded with excitement and would not let the game continue until it had rained $160 in silver on its hero. Big Ed Delahanty of the Phils, a powerhouse who had three over-.400 years and a lifetime average of .346, also belted four in one game two years later. It would not be done again until Lou Gehrig got four—and was robbed of a fifth—in 1932. The hard-drinking Delahanty, the best of five ballplaying brothers, died tragically. Rolling drunk, he evidently tried to walk the international railway bridge across the Niagara River and fell into the torrent.

His teammate and fellow outfielder, Billy Hamilton, was the first to steal more than 100 bases in one season, and went on to steal a respectable 912 in his career. Sliding Billy, however, benefitted from rules that gave runners credit for stolen bases when they stretched a single into a double or went from first to third (an extra base) on a teammate's bingle.

And finally, a record that stood for fifty-nine years: Wee (five-foot, four-and-a-half-inch) Willie Keeler hit safely in forty-four consecutive games. A left-handed batter with a lifetime average of .345, he formulated the place-hitter's basic philosophy: "Hit 'em where they ain't."

Probably the most important event of the decade, however, was the appearance in 1901 of the National League's first and, as it turned out, only enduring rival. The American League was the creation of Byron Bancroft Johnson, a baseball executive of mountainous size, awesome thirst, pompous mien, and the tenacity of a badger. Like many boss men of his time, he was ruthless, crafty, and never forgot or forgave a slight. He did some of his best work under the goad of real or fancied insults.

Ban's transformation of the Western League of 1894 into the American League of 1901 was a masterpiece of wheeling and dealing in which his energies were fired by the scorn, disregard, and resistance of the National League magnates. He immediately placed franchises in three National League strongholds: Chicago, Boston, and Philadelphia. Others went to Washington, Cleveland, and Baltimore. Detroit, a Western League city, continued in place, as did Milwaukee. By 1902, Milwaukee became the Browns and moved into St. Louis to challenge the Cardinals, and, in a complex maneuver, Baltimore invaded New York. This was the linchpin. For if those early Highlanders floundered in the city of the Giants, the time would come when all baseball would have to acknowledge the supremacy of New York's entry in the American League.

Ban built well. He was stuffy and arrogant, but his league organization held together as he had arranged it for more than fifty years. Beyond that, by offering competition to what had formerly been a monopoly, he strengthened the game immeasurably. He kept his owners in line, he backed his umpires to the limit, and as much as anyone he helped bring about the World Series. Best of all, within a few years the American League had Ty Cobb, Tris Speaker, Walter Johnson, Eddie Collins, and more—stars the equal of any.

Top left: *19 Brooklyn Bridegrooms and manager "Bald Billy" Barnie.* Top right: *Fleet Walker (on floor at left) was rare black pro of 1887.* Above: *1894 Orioles. Hanlon (c) has Keeler, Robinson, Jennings on his left. McGraw reclines (l), near Pomeranian mascot.*

15

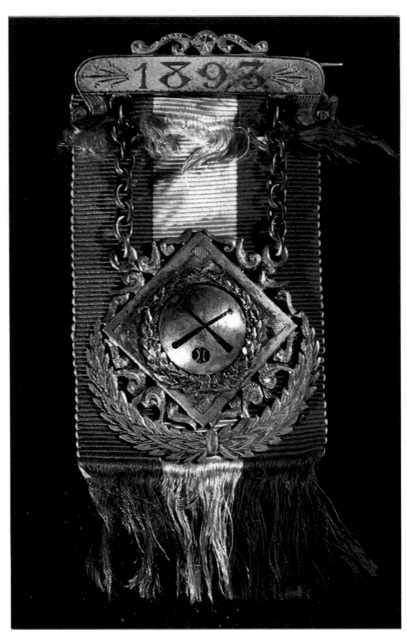

Left: *So-called "cabinet card" portrait of Wilbert Robinson when he was tough, hard-hitting catcher of fabulous Orioles. He once had record seven hits in nine innings. Above: Early press badge. Opposite: Ross Barnes played second base for first great Boston team, jumped to White Stockings in new National League in 1876. In bow tie and high-laced shoes, he is proper figure of an old-time ballplayer.*

16

18

BOSTON

St LOUIS

Die-cut figures of 1880s give clues to players' style but are inaccurate in detail. Boston hitter has foot in bucket and too-short bat. Hard throws must have stung stiff-armed St. Louis first baseman. Indy fielder probably erred often. Chicago pitcher will have no hop on fastball, but until 1884 he had to throw underhand.

1891 Cedar Rapids Baseball Club

Hofer P.　Smith P.　Wittrock P.

Sommers C.F.+C.　Brauty 1st B.　Cedar Mgr.+Capt.　Williams C.

McGraw S.S.　Taylor 2nd B.　Fabian R.F.　Wood L.F.

John J. McGraw, lower left, famous manager of New York Giants and Hall of Famer, played short stop for Cedar Rapids Canaries in 1891. Billy Hofer, upper left, later pitched for the Baltimore Orioles and had a 28-5 record in 1895 and was 26-7 in 1896.

Opposite top: Harper's *sketch of 1874 Red Stockings with bearded captain Harry Wright (c) and Barnes (standing, l). Opposite bottom: Cedar Rapids Canaries of 1891 with 18-year-old shortstop John McGraw (bottom left). By the end of season he had caught on with Baltimore. Billy Hoffer (top left) pitched a few good years for Orioles. Left: Cap Anson, resplendent and assured as leader of White Stockings.* 21

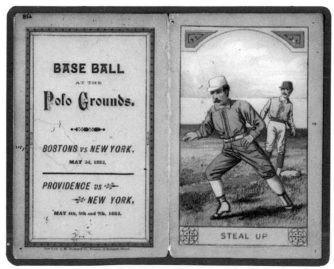

Opposite top: *Album page of 1888-90. Stars, relatively few, were players most often pictured.*
Opposite bottom: *Program for 1883 N.Y. Gothams. Providence games probably pitted Old Hoss Radbourn against Roger Connor, Monte Ward, and Buck Ewing.*
Below: *Modern print of champion St. Louis Browns and their bumptious owner, Chris Von der Ahe, from collection of Charles Comiskey.*
Left: *Big Ed Delahanty, Phils' power hitter, smacked four homers in one game, had several .400 years, hit .346 lifetime.*

Honest   E. J. DELEHANTY.   NEWYORK.

INTERNATIONAL EVENTS

International Tailoring Co. NEW YORK CHICAGO

THE MEN THAT MADE BASE-BALL FAMOUS
The Famous St. Louis Browns (American Assn.) who won the World's Championship Series, 1885-6, from Chicago White Stockings (National League). Photographs from collection of Mr. Chas. A. Comiskey, President White Sox (American League).

How about your FALL CLOTHES?   Get them made-to-measure and give yourself a treat.   See the new beautiful Fall Fabrics.

Above: *Program with ticket stub attached is for 1887 World Series, between Detroit's National League Wolverines and St. Louis Browns of American Association. Browns won 15-game match, played in ten cities.* Right: *Railroad and traction lines promoted Base Ball excursions heavily. Note catcher's primitive mask, pad, and mitt.* Opposite: *Brooklyn park (top) with mannerly crowd rimming outfield, and batter up (bottom) at Pittsburgh's Exposition Park, pre-1909. Topside boxes were best seats in the house.*

BASE BALL

DAWSON
— VS. —
ALBANY

JUNE ✛ 12th

At EXPOSITION GROUNDS,

COLUMBUS, GA

Lovers of Base Ball can witness these games by taking advantage of the very low rates offered by the

COLUMBUS SOUTHERN
❖ RAILWAY ❖

Tickets sold at rates named below, June 12th, will be limited until and good to return on Train leaving Columbus SATURDAY MORNING at 6:25 o'clock.

Electric Cars

Running to Grounds and City, will meet Train at Union Depot on arrival. Fare to Grounds, or any part of the City, only 5 cents.

ROUND TRIP RATES.

From ALBANY	$1 00	From RICHLAND	$ 75
" DAWSON	75	" BROOKLYN	75
" PARROTTS	75	" RENFROE	75
" WESTON	75	" CUSSETA	75

❖SCHEDULES❖

ALBANY	Leave 6:30 A. M.	WESTON	Leave 8:19 A. M.
SASSER	7:11	RICHLAND	8:45 "
DAWSON	7:31	CUSSETA	9:39 "
PARROTTS	7:54	COLUMBUS	Arrive 10:30 "

RETURNING Train will leave COLUMBUS at 6:00 P. M.

JOHN ESCRIDGE, HENRY WOOTEN, JOHN ANDERSON,
MANAGERS.

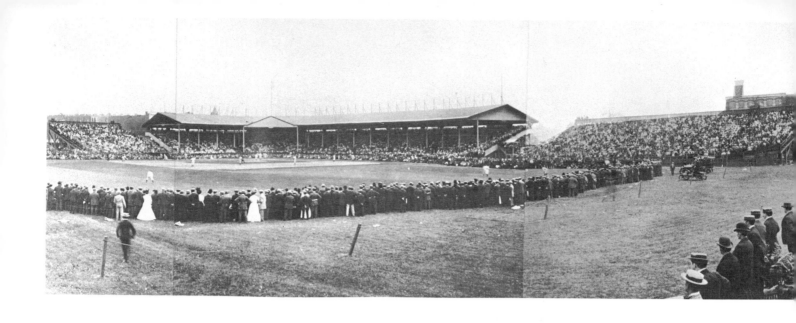

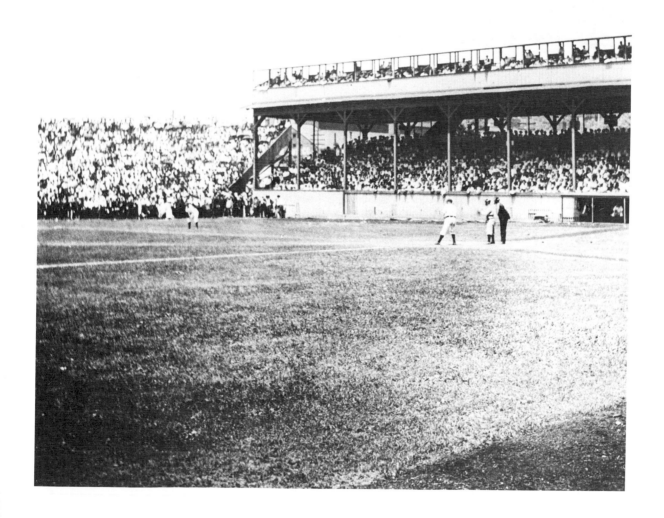

25

Right *and* below: *As baseball's lively
new vocabulary entered the language,
baseball situations became a
never-ending source of humor, as
cartoon cards suggest. Opposite:
Bat, button, and scorecard,
all of 1880s. Bat is slightly
tapered, but handle is fat, barrel
slender. Stripe decoration
must have been general. It's in
drawing on page 24. Past
century, lacking today's many ad
media, was big for buttons.
This one advertises cereal. See
familiar Y-struts of stands in
background. Program is for Reds'
1888 season in American Association.
Kid Baldwin was their catcher.*

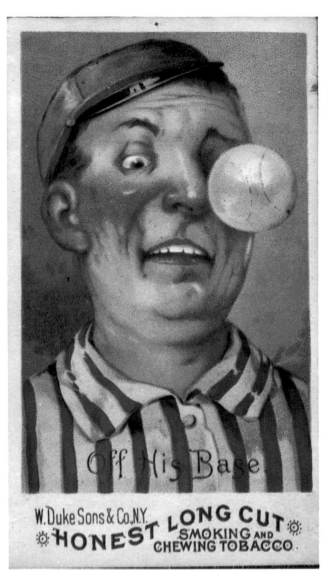

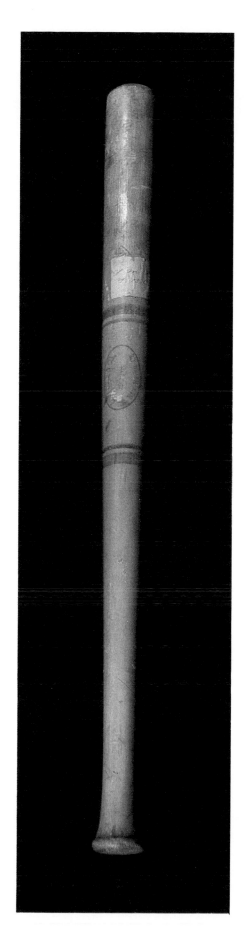

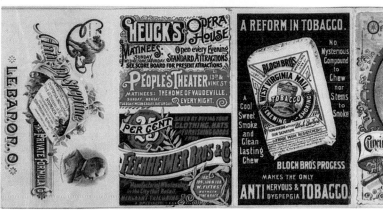

Chapter 2

THE AGE OF McGRAW 1901·1913

Baseball entered the modern era when John McGraw came to New York to manage the Giants in 1902. He did not transform the game all by himself. Many movers and shakers had a hand in that: his longtime managerial rivals, Connie Mack and Frank Chance, great players like Ty Cobb and Honus Wagner, and, for all his cantankerousness and bullheadedness, Ban Johnson. Yet by the stamp and impress of his personality on the game, McGraw was paramount even in this brilliant company. His achievement was in setting a tone and establishing a style, and in bringing major league status to the nation's number-one city by making his Giants winners. When "Laughing Larry" Doyle, the ebullient second baseman, said, "Gee, it's great to be young and a Giant!" much of America could agree that he did, indeed, enjoy two of life's more enviable blessings.

The Giants, in existence for twenty-one years, had known few moments of glory before McGraw took over. There were two pennants in the 1880s under Jim Mutrie, who is credited with originating the team's nickname ("My big boys. My giants," he said fondly), and another, in 1894, under John Montgomery Ward. This had been a sentimental triumph, for Monte, a member of the mail-order clan, was one of the grand old-timers of the league, a pitcher of renown who later became an equally fine shortstop, second baseman, and outfielder.

Since then, the Giants had been sinking to the bottom of the league, losing stars at each stage of the descent. Roger Connor, the redoubtable first baseman, was gone. So was Buck Ewing, and so, too, the tireless arms of Tim Keefe, Mickey Welch, and Amos Rusie. In the winning years of '88 and '89, Keefe and Welch had pitched 116 of the team's 163 victories.

McGraw came aboard when the 1902 season was more than half over and two previous managers already had been fired. He could not keep the team from finishing eighth and last, but he brought along five players from Baltimore, now in the American League, to put some of that famous Oriole ginger into his flaccid Giants. One, an untried youth, was the excellent Roger Bresnahan, an outfielder who had not yet discovered what a fine catcher he was. Another was a veteran right-handed pitcher named Joe McGinnity. The Iron Man would win 143 games for McGraw in the next six years. Two pretty fair pitchers already were on hand: Luther Taylor, a deaf mute known in the affectionately brutal humor of the time as "Dummy," and a third-year man named Christy Mathewson. A collegian from Bucknell, in Pennsylvania, he had come to the attention of Connie Mack's Athletics, but had slipped away and been signed by the Giants. One of the phenomenal pitchers of all time, he would win 177 games in the next six years (and 373 throughout his career), so he and Iron Man would account for fifty-six percent of the team's victories in that time. Can anyone imagine what the A's would have been like if Mathewson had joined Plank, Bender, and Waddell?

Within a year or so, almost no one who had been part of the losing tradition remained with the Giants. In 1903 they shot up to second place. In 1904 they won the pennant by a sixteen-game margin over Frank Chance's Cubs. Although the initial World Series had been played in 1903, antipathy toward the upstart American League still ran strong in the National, and McGraw would not allow his new champions to meet the Red Sox.

*Most valuable of
all picture cards is
Wagner item from T-206
American Tobacco
Trust series of 1909-10.
When Honus found he
was endorsing the weed,
he had card withdrawn.
Very few survived.*

Winners again in 1905, the Giants relented and played the A's. This was the famous Series in which all games were shutouts: three by Matty, one by McGinnity, and one by Chief Bender. Rube Waddell, the wonderful and eccentric left-hander, did not play. In one of the escapades that tried Connie Mack's patience so sorely, the Rube was injured in a scuffle while trying to bust pitcher Andy Coakley's out-of-season straw hat. As luck would have it, this was the one year in Waddell's up-and-down career when he could have pitched in a Series. Matty would have other Series but none better. In engineering his three shutouts—three complete games in six days—he allowed only fourteen hits, one walk, and struck out eighteen. A sartorial note: The Giants were freshly outfitted for the occasion. They appeared in crisp, new black uniforms with white trim, a startling sight, especially to the A's in their heavy, sweat-soaked, seldom-laundered flannels, the standard garb of the time.

If there was any doubt before, it now was clear that the Age of McGraw had dawned. In the eleven years from 1903 through 1913, his Giants finished first or second nine times. (In the twenty-three years from 1903 through 1925, they were first or second nineteen times!) They had become the kingpins of the National League and Little Mac was their absolute monarch.

He was tough, truculent, and imperious, humorless and uncharming. The stories about him all have to do with his drill-sergeant domination of his players (i.e., fining the man who swung away and got an important hit when the signal from the bench had been to sacrifice) or his provoking, challenging, intimidating antics on the field. He was a superb tactician, alert to every nuance of the clever, scrambling, one-run-at-a-time baseball of his era. He called pitches, signaled batters, maneuvered fielders, baited umpires, feuded with rival owners, and antagonized crowds in every city of the circuit.

He was not easy to like and encouraged no intimacies, yet he was fair with his players and they respected and obeyed him. He stoutly defended the two Freds—Merkle and Snodgrass—after they committed the two costliest errors in Giant history. (Or three. Merkle, whose failure to touch second in 1908 helped lose a pennant to the Cubs, also helped lose the 1912 Series. After Snodgrass's famous seventh-game dropped fly, Merkle let Speaker's pop foul fall untouched near first base. Reprieved, Spoke singled in the tying run and a sacrifice fly scored the winner.) Like all hard men Mac had his soft spots. He loved Matty, as he later loved Mel Ott, for the uniqueness of his talent, his competitive fire, and his decency.

Off the field he was a roisterer. He was a partner in a saloon, played the horses, traveled with the sporting crowd. But baseball was never absent from his thoughts. When his Giants fell into a slump, he jolted them out of it by paying a teamster to drive a wagonload of empty barrels, a surefire omen of base hits to come, past the Polo Grounds.

People who remember the tired, ailing, muffin-faced old man who resigned his beloved Giants to Bill Terry in 1932 may find all this brilliance hard to believe. But it was there. And his winning percentage of .589 for thirty-three years has been exceeded by only one other long-term manager in the history of the game—Joe McCarthy.

There was excitement in the American League, too, at first merely from the fact of its existence, then on its own merits. Many of its early stars—Cy Young, Clark Griffith, Nap Lajoie, Jimmy Collins—jumped from the older league, but within a few years it was growing its own.

Furthermore, major league ball was new to such growing American League cities as Cleveland, Milwaukee, Detroit, and Washington, and crowds turned out. In the league's first year, attendance ran fewer than 300,000 behind the National League and in 1902 went half a million ahead.

What established American League parity as much as anything probably was the World Series of 1906, an all-Chicago contest in which the White Sox, known to history as "the Hitless Wonders," polished off the Cubs, one of the great teams of all time. The Sox were, indeed, Wonders, even in those weak-hitting days. The team batting average was .230. Pitching carried them: Big Ed Walsh, Doc White, and Nick Altrock, who did a clown baseball act with Al Schacht many years later, but was then a tough, twenty-one-game winner with a good move that kept runners anchored to first.

No one thought they had a chance against the Cubs, who had played .763 ball in winning 116 games and had finished twenty games ahead of the Giants. They led the National League in batting, fielding, most runs scored, fewest runs allowed, most shutouts, and most strikeouts, and had a staff earned-run average of 1.76. Tinker to Evers to Chance were a memorable infield combination, and the team's leading hitter, Harry Steinfeldt, was at third. "Wildfire" Frank Schulte was in right. Johnny Kling caught. Mordecai ("Three-finger") Brown led the six-man pitching staff with twenty-six wins, twenty-seven complete games, and a 1.04 ERA.

The teams split the first four games, typical low-scoring affairs. Ed Reulbach and Brown threw one- and two-hitters for the Cubs, Walsh a two-hitter for the Sox. Then the hitless ones exploded for twenty-six hits in the last two games, winning both for the championship.

Notwithstanding the occasional outburst of scoring, the Age of McGraw was essentially an Age of Pitching. No other era has had so many glittering performers, so many lifetime winners of more than 200 games. Everyone knows the famous ones: Cy Young, Johnson, Mathewson, and Alexander. You may have to stretch to recall Red Faber of the White Sox, Jack Quinn of the Yanks, Red Sox, and A's, and the marvelously named Eppa Jephtha Rixey, who won 266 for the Phils and Reds. And you really know your baseball if you know the Pirates' Vic Willis, a 248-game winner, or Jack Powell, a well-traveled right-hander and an oddity. Jack is one of two pitchers with more than 200 victories who lost more than he won: 247-254 between 1897 and 1912. The other: the ineffable "Bobo" Newsom.

These were the stars with the most imposing career records, but both leagues were full of men a few wins shy of two hundred, or who performed brilliantly for a few seasons: the Red Sox' sore-armed Joe Wood who was 34-5 in 1912, Dick Rudolph of the Braves, Ed Walsh, Ed Reulbach, Jeff Tesreau, Babe Adams, Ernie Shore, Nap Rucker, Orvie Overall, Jack Coombs. And how about Tom Seaton? Tom Seaton? He won twenty-seven for the Phils in 1913 and twenty-five for the Brooklyn Federal League team in 1914.

Two Ty Cobb cards from early phase of his amazing career. Colorful cabinet card is at top. *Smaller cigarette card,* above, *does not quite show hands-apart batting grip.*

31

Jimmy Collins, top, was one of first fine-fielding third basemen. Eddie Collins card, above, is rare, unissued item from T-206 series.

To be precise, the Age of Pitching began in 1903 and extended through 1919, to the Ruthian Era. Three factors were responsible for it: the ball was dead, rules and game conditions favored pitchers, and big swingers were few. The ball simply had no resilience, no carry. Strong men could whack it with big, wagon-tongue bats and get nothing more than a long single. Tris Speaker's notable talent for playing a shallow center field is evidence of this. He parked himself twenty yards or so behind second, where he could catch what eventually came to be called "Titanics"—sinking liners—over the infielders' heads, or field a ground single before the hitter could grab an extra base, or race back for a beautiful, over-the-shoulder catch of anything that got tagged hard. Not many fielders could do it, of course. You had to be fast, get the jump, and be an excellent judge of a fly ball. Still, the fact that it was possible at all meant that Spoke could be sure that few hitters were going to larrup one over his head.

Many fewer balls were used, too. Umpires did not put a new one in play until the game ball had been scuffed, dirtied, grass-stained, and just about battered out of shape. Such balls were harder to see, soggier to hit, and more likely to behave eccentrically in flight.

What the course of the game did not do to the ball wily pitchers did. For one favorite pitch or another they scuffed it with sandpaper (emery ball), smoothed a patch with talcum or paraffin (shine ball), loaded it with spit, nicked the cover, stained it with tobacco juice. Doctoring made the ball curve, drop, sail, or slide in ways exasperating to hitters, who had trouble enough with Matty's "fadeaway" (a right-hander's in-curve; today the screwball), Russell Ford's "fork ball" (a change-up), or routine fastballs and curves. Spitters curved more wickedly than usual because of the wet spot on the ball. Pitchers who relied on it heavily were well advised to chew tobacco to keep the saliva flowing, or a fine native product called slippery elm, the demulcent inner bark of a species of elm tree.

As if this were not enough, since 1901 a batter's first two fouls had been counted as strikes. Previously they had been ignored. Only whiffs or called strikes counted. This gave a new and unaccustomed edge to pitchers, whose strike zone, incidentally, was somewhat larger than today's.

No wonder there were few good hitters. Analysis of the lineups of the sixteen major league clubs between 1901 and 1920 shows that amazingly anemic batting averages were the rule. Seasons went by in which there were only six or seven .300 hitters in an entire league.

Looking back, much of this futility is obscured by the fact that Wagner, Cobb, Eddie Collins, and Nap Lajoie—the great natural hitters—were banging the ball at .350 or better, while Chance, Mike Donlin, Fred Clarke, Cy Seymour, "Home Run" Baker, Keeler, Ginger Beaumont, Sherry Magee, Sam Crawford, and Steinfeldt could be counted on for .300-.333 seasons as often as not. These were the few consistent and successful hitters.

Perhaps anyone but the best had to have had trouble. For if conditions favored the pitchers, it was also true that the pitchers were superb. Moreover, these were pitchers who *worked*. Year after year, entire seasons were pitched by staffs of five or six men. The pennant-winning 1907 Tigers got 113 complete games and 135 decisions from just four men!

Yet the physiology of shoulders and elbows has not changed since 1910, and throwing a baseball a hundred or more times an afternoon takes its toll. There were sore arms in the old days, too, Joe Wood's perhaps the most famous.

Interestingly, even after they enlivened the ball in 1911, things didn't change very much. The ball was given a cork center encased in a one-eighth-inch rubber layer. There was an immediate jump in the number of .300 hitters to thirty-seven. Cobb hit .420 and Joe Jackson .408. (Joe wasn't happy. He hit .408, .395, and .373 in his first three full seasons and didn't win a thing, because Cobb hit .420, .410, and .390.) Still, the pitchers continued to dominate. There were twelve or fourteen twenty-game winners every year and many ERAs stayed below 2. As time went on, the .300 hitters dwindled, not to the pre-1911 level, but to fewer than twenty.

Perhaps a great many pitchers simply were outstanding. In more recent times, only the likes of Lefty Grove, Newson, Early Wynn, Warren Spahn, Jim Bunning, Don Drysdale, the Perrys, and Bob Gibson have shown us what those old-time rubber arms must have been like.

Those turn-of-the-century players weren't great fielders either—statistically, at any rate. With very few exceptions, the top fifteen all-time fielding averages at each position are held by players active since World War II. This is interesting, because you would assume that bunts, slap hits, choked bats, dead balls, and so forth would mean a slower, more reachable, fieldable ball. Gloves, of course, were primitive. As late as 1909 they still had no webbing between thumb and fingers. And some fields evidently were in terrible shape. Cobb said the outfields he played on often had ruts, rough spots, and long grass, particularly in Detroit during the regime of penny-pinching Frank Navin. Although Tyrus was a bit prone to both complaint and exaggeration, he was not the only one to say so. Honus Wagner was famous for steamshovel hands that gathered ground balls, dirt, and gravel like a scoop and fired them all, indiscriminately, toward first. This suggests something about the playing surfaces around short.

At the same time, rising profits from increasing crowds encouraged all clubs to begin replacing their decrepit, nineteenth-century wooden grandstands. The A's and the Pirates were first to build modern, steel-and-concrete stadiums: Shibe Park and Forbes Field, in 1909. Forbes, erected in the fashionable Schenley Park district, was a double-decker with a row of boxes on top. It had elevators, ramps, electric lights, and telephones—marvels for a ball park—and was served by a complex of trolley lines. Fans could get a round-trip fare and a ticket to the game for 60¢. Griffith Stadium, Cleveland's League Park, Comiskey Park, the new Polo Grounds (after the old one burned down) came along soon after. With all this modernity, and more to come, the fields must have been in reasonable condition.

So it may be that fielding is one area in which modern ballplayers could give the old guys lessons. It is a well-demonstrated fact that Tinker, Evers, and Chance were not really adept at the double play. "Prince Hal" Chase was celebrated as a graceful first baseman, yet even he was terrible. He is not in the top fifteen for lifetime averages or assists. He led the league in errors in eight of the fifteen years he played and generally fielded in the

Sheet music celebrates Hitless Wonders.

33

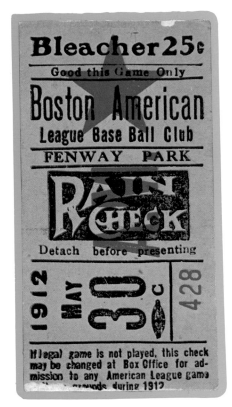

.970s and .980s, about par for a second baseman. As everyone knows, errors may mean extra effort to snag the hard chance, although in Chase's case this would be an ironic excuse considering the miasma of deliberate errors and thrown games that hovered over the man throughout his career.

As a matter of fact, few infielders of the time were noted for adroit play as, in more recent times, Red Schoendienst, Phil Rizzuto, or Brooks Robinson have been. Jimmy Collins of the Red Sox could come in fast for a bunt toward third. Who else? Rabbit Maranville perhaps. Most praise was reserved for dashing outfielders.

Still, it was—as it still is—a lovely game to see. Old-time fans were real enthusiasts and formed societies to root their favorites on. The Red Sox had their Royal Rooters, the White Sox their Woodland Bards. They sang songs to the music of hired bands, they were boisterous and very visible, particularly in enemy territory at World Series time.

Squads were smaller. Team pictures usually show twenty or twenty-one men, sometimes more, but often fewer. Aside from eight regulars and six pitchers, there would be a second catcher, three or four utility men, perhaps a fading star playing part-time at his old position, and a couple of extra pitchers for the odd game. There was little tampering with lineups. Regulars won their positions and their places in the batting order in the spring and kept them, barring injury, until season's end.

In the early days the players dressed at their hotels (top hotels, incidentally, not fleabags, as some seem to think) and were driven to the park in horse-drawn carriages. McGraw made sure the Giants' carts were embla-

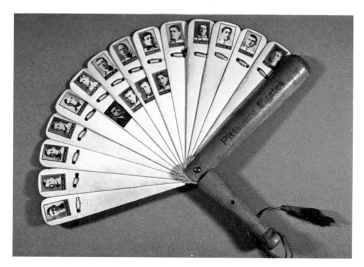

Opposite top and bottom left: *For a quarter you could see Tris Speaker at Fenway, for 50¢ Nap Rucker at Brooklyn. Opposite right: Fan's program notes that Cobb and Tigers trounced Highlanders en route to 1907 pennant. Mementos took many forms. Left: Bat breaks to reveal pictures of 1907 Pirates. Below: Matty adorns baseball-shaped Giant fan.*

A FAN for A FAN

Christy Mathewson

zoned with signs and banners proclaiming their presence; no skulking through Chicago and Cincinnati for him. Visiting players might be cheered, importuned for autographs, or, if they had trounced the home nine, pelted with fruits and vegetables. By 1906 the National League required all parks to provide visiting-team dressing rooms with lockers and hot showers. The American followed suit soon after.

Games started at 3 or 3:30. The Giants, presumably catering to the Stock Exchange crowd, had a 4 P.M. starting time until 1912. Prices varied from place to place and time to time, but generally bleacher tickets were 25¢, general admission 50¢, boxes $1. An array of food and drink was available.

Players' uniforms changed style slowly. The buttoned high collar continued to about 1913, then gave way to the open-necked shirt. Sleeves were half or three-quarter length. For cold weather, clubs issued heavy cardigan sweaters with a shawl collar and a simple team emblem. Caps were skimpy, except for the boxy ones favored by the A's—very much like those of today's Pirates. By 1910 or so, pull-down sunglasses with smoked lenses were attached to the bill. White home uniforms and gray ones for the road were introduced about the same time.

Almost anything that happened was new. The first official statistical reports on games were compiled for the leagues in 1903. The pregame batting and fielding drills were formalized in 1906. Roger Bresnahan is generally credited with introducing shin guards for catchers in 1907.

Spring training began in mid-February and included a thirty- or forty-game exhibition schedule as the teams worked their way north. At first the teams ventured only about as far as South Carolina. The Giants used Marlin, Texas, near the Brazos River, for a dozen years, but by 1911 Florida began to be the major site.

Other than keep—$6 a day—players got no money until the season began in mid-April. A good standard salary was $3,000. Outstanding players made $4,000 to $5,000. Superstars did better, though not remarkably so. Mathewson was still making $8,000 in his twelfth year with the Giants. Cobb worked his figure up to $9,000 after twice winning the American League batting crown. By comparison, blue-collar workers in many industries made less than $1,000 a year.

Travel was done by train. The 154-game schedule was well established (11 games at home and 11 away with each of the seven other clubs), so travel was considerable, and slow. Boston to St. Louis was a sixteen-hour journey. Road trips (a three- or four-game series in each city) could take three weeks. Railroads and hotels were pleased to have baseball business and players went first class. They chatted, played cards, snoozed on trains. Boisterous ones drank and raised hell. Rookies were told that the green netting slung in Pullman berths to hold incidentals was to rest their valuable throwing arms. Country boys who believed everything they heard awoke with a crick in their neck next morning. Ha-ha!

It was a pretty good life. Owners were not notably generous, and several were outrageous skinflints, yet they probably didn't treat their workers any worse than other bosses of the time. Most players went along, and as no one ever tired of telling them, you couldn't beat the hours.

Above: *Rube Waddell, when he was with A's. Rube could have been greater than he was.* Opposite: *Hans Wagner relaxes on Pirate equipment trunk. Bat and spikes have modern look, but collar and sleeve are still in old-fashioned style.*

. SAFE AT THIRD

TRYING TO CATCH HIM NAPPING

*A gallery of 1911 cabinet cards. Top:
Giant slides under throw to Bobby Byrne
in smoky Pittsburgh. Above: Red beats
pickoff toss to Fred Merkle. Opposite:
Brooklyn's Tim Jordan, like all
right-handed first basemen, has trouble
making tag (on Giants' Buck Herzog), bottom.
Top left: Wahoo Sam played outfield with
Cobb. Top right: Big Ed, White Sox mainstay.*

CRAWFORD Detroit

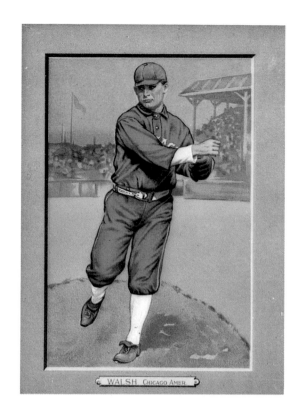

WALSH Chicago Amer

JORDAN & HERZOG AT FIRST

Opposite top: *Forbes Field opening in 1909 as first steel-&-concrete stadium. It had ramps, phones, rooftop boxes, and trolley service to front door. League Park (opposite bottom),* Indians' *new home, was cramped for space from outset.* Above: *Fans arriving at Braves Field;* left: *overflow Series crowd at Philadelphia's tiny Baker Bowl.*

Above: *Giants' Doyle raps hit for Boston Garter.* Right: *Strip of Hassan "triples"— two players plus action photo of game. Opposite top: T-205's of 1911 have printing error (red sock) on one Pat Dougherty card. Lower right is Cubs' Orvie Overall. Opposite bottom: Backs of T-209 series.*

WALTER JOHNSON

Opposite (clockwise from top): *Cubs' Harry Steinfeldt in batting practice, 1908 (catcher disdaining newfangled shin guards); Matty warming up at Polo Grounds for fifth game of 1913 World Series (he lost); young Walter Johnson threw fastest fastball. Above: 1907 Tigers won pennant. Left: 1910 Cubs took fourth flag for Chance.*

THE TIP-TOP BOY MASCOT

PLANK, PHILA. AMER.

Opposite top: *Picture-card series. 1910 minor leaguers included Iron Man McGinnity and Ping Bodie.* Opposite left: *Mascot touted Tip-Top bread of Ward sports tycoons.* Opposite right: *Eddie Plank card, T-206 series, is rare and valuable.* Above: *1912 series with Buck Weaver, Grover Lowdermilk, Max Carey, Paddy Livingston (of A's and Indians), and Terry Turner came in Recruit little-cigar boxes.*

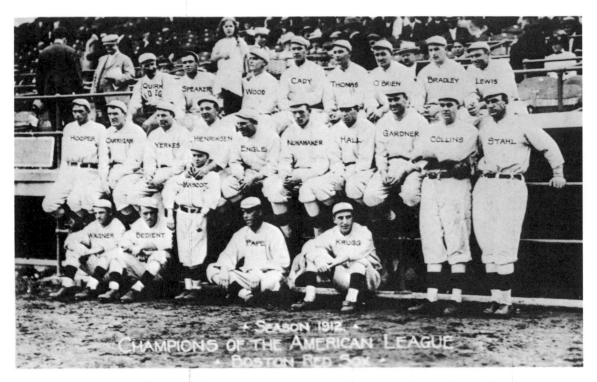

Top: *Red Sox of 1912 beat Giants in 7-game Series as Joe Wood, winner of 34 games in regular season, took three. Manager Jake Stahl is at right. Collins is pitcher Ray. Above: Fan dates around 1907; pictures are sixteen all-stars.* Right: *Cub promotion piece of 1908.* Opposite: *Variety of picture-card games from 1890s to 1913.*

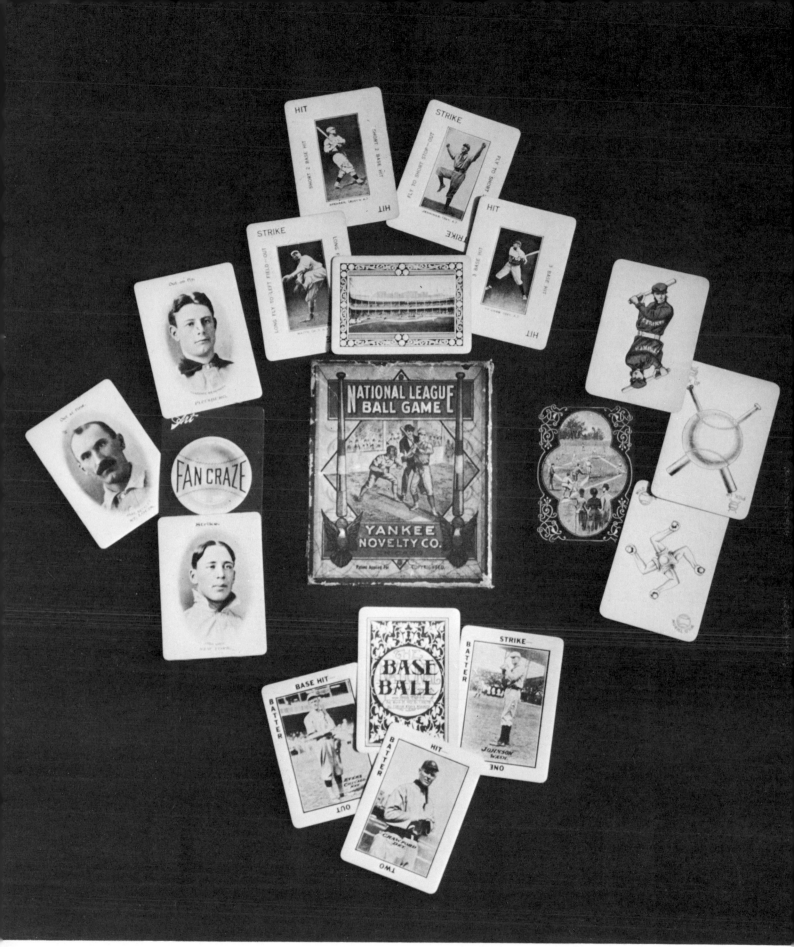

THE MOEHLE LITHOGRAPHIC CO.
CLARENDON ROAD & E. 37TH ST. BROOKLYN, N.Y.
BRANCH OFFICE: 170 W. RANDOLPH ST. CHICAGO, ILL.

NO. 843	INS	$1.80	PER 100
NO. 844	OUTS	.90	" "
NO. 845	TAG	.50	" "
NO. 846	B.W.F.	.35	" "

ALSO BLANK

STAR PLAY

*Particular poses showed up
often in early days.
Silk pillow cover, left, has
familiar representations of
Cobb (see page 31), Matty,
and Speaker, plus Ed Walsh and
Home Run Baker. Opposite:* Famous
*photo of Rube Marquard is
printed on cloth. Above:* Star
Play *label on cigar-box lid
shows lively, if inaccurate,
idea of game. Shortstop
will regret barehanded stab
of liner. Slider must have
gotten big jump on ball,
runner to third none at all.*

51

Chapter 3

TIME OF TURMOIL 1914-1919

These six years were a time of turmoil for baseball and for the larger world beyond its grandstands and fences. They were the period of World War I, an involvement at first remote from all Americans and eventually one that demanded that everyone, ballplayers too, "work or fight." They saw four of the preeminent clubs of the previous decade—the Athletics, Tigers, Cubs, and Pirates—lose their momentum and drop out of contention. In the National League four upstarts—Boston, Philadelphia, Brooklyn, and Cincinnati—suddenly became pennant winners. In the American they were glory years for the Red Sox, infamous ones for the A's, who were so ruthlessly dismantled by Connie Mack that it would take fifteen years to get them back on top.

It was a period that endured the short, interesting, expensive, and disruptive life of the Federal League.

And it ended with the shock and shame of a corrupt World Series.

Yet in the view of many, these years, and the three or four immediately preceding them, were also a Golden Age, a classical period when baseball was played as well as it will ever be played, when it achieved an optimum balance of offense and defense, an equilibrium among its many skills. In today's terms play was perhaps a bit austere. Pitching still had the edge over hitting. The great ones continued to hit remarkably for average, but homers were few and not even especially admired. It was a comparatively short-range game of bunts, steals, sacrifices, strategic singles, scoring flies, squeeze plays, the hit-and-run, plus a few extra-base hits to loosen things up and keep everybody honest.

It was the noonday of the stolen base. Every team in both leagues stole more than one hundred per season, the faster, more adroit teams more than two hundred. Between 1911 and 1920 the sixteen major league clubs stole 26,734 bases. (That's seven thousand more than the twenty- and twenty-four-team majors stole between 1966 and 1975!) Everyone ran, even Ping Bodie, the slow, heavy, and popular outfielder of the White Sox, A's, and Yanks. Observing Ping thrown out at second, Bugs Baer reported, "His heart was full of larceny, but his feet were honest."

Cobb, Wagner, Speaker, Mathewson, Johnson, and Eddie Collins still performed prodigiously, but Cy Young, Nap Lajoie, Willie Keeler, and others who had begun playing in the nineteenth century were reaching the end of the line. Henceforward, every young ballplayer would be a child of the twentieth century.

As always, extraordinary youngsters were coming along, their arrival and success perhaps causing more of a stir than is customary today because the scouting and development of players was more haphazard and less well publicized. "Rough" Carrigan, the Red Sox manager, knew he was getting a prize when Babe Ruth came up in mid-1914, but the kid's strong, left-handed pitching was a revelation to Boston fans in his first full season the next year. The Browns, through the artful maneuvering of their field manager, Branch Rickey, acquired George Sisler, about to become one of the three or four best first basemen of all time. The Cardinals came up with Rogers Hornsby, eventually the game's most formidable right-handed batter. And Cleveland had an illiterate South Carolinian in the outfield: Joe Jackson, a superb natural hitter whose swing had a grace and purity that baseball

Home Run Baker in Yankee pinstripes takes pregame batting practice in oldtime cage, around 1917.

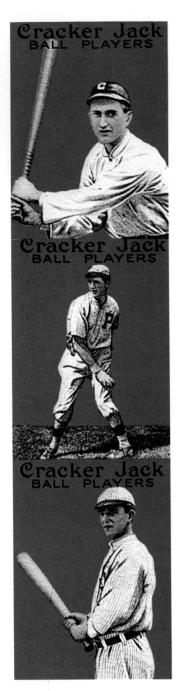

Cracker Jack series of 1915 shows above, top to bottom: *Shoeless Joe Jackson just before trade to White Sox, Alexander in first of three 30-win seasons, and scrappy receiver Ray Schalk.*

men remembered and marveled at long after "the Shoeless One" was gone.

The Dodgers had a hero in Zack Wheat, earnest, accomplished, and steady. This was the first of Wilbert Robinson's eighteen years as Brooklyn's manager. He would have few moments of glory and many of confusion, but he would be regarded by long-suffering Ebbets Field loyalists with sardonic affection and his floundering teams would be called Robins.

In the spring of 1914, those perennial rivals, the Athletics and the Giants, were the reigning powers of the major leagues. The A's were world champions and favored to repeat. The Giants, who had won three straight pennants (and lost three Series), might well take a fourth.

Baseball's routine was upset, however, and its atmosphere troubled, by the appearance of the Federal League, a third eight-team circuit aspiring to major status. "Outlaws!" cried the Nationals and Americans, which was nonsense. No one had a patent on the game, and if Harry Sinclair, the oil millionaire, Phil Ball, the ice magnate, the brothers Ward of the bakery fortune, and other moneybags wanted a league of their own, there was nothing to stop them.

In truth their structure was a rickety one. They established clubs in four big-league cities—Chicago, St. Louis, Pittsburgh, and Brooklyn—and four more marginal areas—Baltimore, Buffalo, Indianapolis, and Kansas City. Joe Tinker managed the Chifeds. Mordecai Brown bossed the St. Louis Terriers, or, less felicitously, the Sloufeds. Bill Bradley, formerly Cleveland's ace third baseman, ran the Tip Tops, named for the Wards' brand of bread, or Brookfeds. Every club had a name player or two who had jumped his National or American League team: Bill McKechnie, about to get his first taste of managing, Claude Hendrix, Jack Quinn, Russell Ford, Tom Seaton, Doc Crandall, Al Bridwell, Hy Myers, and Hal Chase, who never could resist spitting in the Establishment's eye. These were good enough names. There just weren't enough of them. Rosters had to be filled out with minor leaguers and free agents.

Even so, the wonder was that desertions weren't wholesale. The reserve clause, which gave clubs endlessly renewable options on players' services, plus the majors' monopoly control of the game's apparatus, made players' salaries a take-it-or-leave-it proposition. Now, to repel the free-spending Federal raiders and hold their teams together, the majors had to start paying real money. Many salaries were doubled. For a brief, horrifying moment even the peerless Walter Johnson yielded to the smell of money and defected. His $10,000 was a regal salary for the time, but he had won thirty-four and twenty-eight games in 1913 and 1914, and when Clark Griffith refused his terms for the next year, "the Big Train" signed a three-year pact with the Chifeds. Griffith hastened to Johnson's home in Kansas, sweetened his offer, and persuaded the greatest chattel he would ever own to break his contract with the Feds.

Once the season was underway, it was clear that the new league was mediocre at best, but its presence was costly. When admissions were cut to 25¢ and even 10¢ to draw fans, the Nationals and Americans in competing cities had to follow suit. If the Feds were hurting, so were the majors and the high minors whose territory was invaded.

Meanwhile, the Athletics were moving confidently toward another pennant. The famous $100,000 infield—Stuffy McInnis, Collins, Jack Barry, and Frank Baker—made Philadelphia the best fielding team in the league. A brilliant seven-man pitching staff, with Bob Shawkey and "Bullet Joe" Bush taking some of the load off Plank and Bender, won frequently.

In the National League a miracle was in progress. On July 4, halfway through the season, the Boston Braves were eighth, eleven games behind the first-place Reds. They were playing sluggish ball—thirty-five won and forty-three lost—and appeared to be hopelessly out of the race. But they were about to embark on one of the more exciting runs for the flag the National League had ever seen. It is often pointed out that the league was actually rather closely bunched and that the Braves didn't have overly much ground to make up. True. But they still won sixty of their next seventy-three games, a fantastic winning percentage of .789.

For all that, it was a patchwork team that got mileage from good defense, good pitching, and intangibles—the imaginative and emotional leadership of manager George Stallings and the impetus that a hot streak always gives a club.

Johnny Evers, "the Crab," winding down his career but still a hard loser, came from Chicago to fire up his new mates, as Eddie Stanky, another scrapper, would do for the Braves of 1948. Rabbit Maranville, a wizened youth who drank and played ball with equal pleasure for more than twenty years, was at short. He caught all pop flies at his belt buckle, much as Willie Mays did, although even more startlingly, because on those straight-up, straight-down infield hits the ball looked as though it would scrape the letters off his chest before plummeting into the glove. He and Evers were a good combination. The Braves led the league in double plays.

Otherwise, it was an ordinary club. They platooned at third and used eleven outfielders in the course of the season, trying to find the right three. Fortunately, they had three superb pitchers, one more than the Braves of '48. Dick Rudolph (27-10) had the best of his thirteen major league years, Bill James (26-7), the only good one of his short career, and George Tyler (16-14) supplied left-handed strength. They pitched eighty-two complete games. Most miraculously, the Braves were irresistible in the Series. They shocked the A's with a four-game sweep.

Connie Mack thereupon destroyed his team. Deliberately, implacably, he scattered his four-time pennant winners to the winds. What nihilistic spirit moved the kindly Connie to this act of vandalism? Throughout his long baseball life he was pinched financially and explained many of his drastic actions as answering a need for cash; in 1914 he said it was the increased payroll forced on him by the Federal League. Perhaps. But it is hard to see how he figured it was better to have $50,000 than Eddie Collins, the first of the stars he unloaded.

The A's fell like a rock to the bottom of the league in 1915. They scored the fewest runs of any American League team and allowed the most. They made the most errors, had the worst team fielding average, and the next-to-worst batting average. They lost 109 games and finished 58½ behind the Red Sox. It was the first of seven straight years in the cellar.

Top to bottom: *Branch Rickey, Browns' manager, marvelous Mordecai Brown, and Rabbit Maranville. Oddly, weak-hitting Rabbit had more lifetime triples than Musial, Ruth, Gehrig, or Hornsby.*

Tickets to Disaster: confused, corrupt clash of Cincinnati and Chicago in 1919. Game 3 was straight. Dickie Kerr, one of the Clean Sox, shut out Reds, 3-0. Game 4 was crooked. Reds won, 2-0, on two errors by Eddie Cicotte.

There were other turns of the wheel by which titans of past years were overtaken and surpassed. The Pirates fell into the second division. The Cubs won only one pennant between 1910 and 1929, the Tigers none between 1909 and 1934. Even the Giants, while consistently a first-division team, had only one pennant between 1913 and 1921, and managed to finish last in 1915. Of course, being the Giants they were the best eighth-place team in history, playing .454 ball and only three-and-a-half games out of fourth. (Their record finally was topped in 1975, when the Cubs and Astros finished last in the National League East at .463.)

The New York Yankees—everyone had stopped calling them the Highlanders—changed hands in 1915. A worn-out franchise with a collapsing plant and a losing team, it was picked up for under half a million by Jacob Ruppert, brewer and society swell, and his friend Tillinghast L'Hommedieu Huston, an engineer-contractor who made his pile in Cuba after the Spanish-American War. It took a while to turn things around, but when they did the improvement was marked and long term to the point of permanence.

For the Red Sox these were perhaps the peak years. They won pennants and world championships in 1915, 1916, and 1918, and finished second in 1914 and 1917. The Royal Rooters preened. They had perhaps the finest outfield in baseball: Speaker in center, Duffy Lewis playing Fenway's short left field with its sloping embankment, and Harry Hooper in right. Their only challengers were Detroit's Cobb, Bobby Veach, and "Wahoo Sam" Crawford or, when Wahoo wore out, Harry Heilmann. The Tigers may have been heavier hitters, but the Sox exceeded them as fielders.

In 1915 Boston won a close race with the Tigers and went on to beat the Phillies of Grover Cleveland Alexander and Gavvy Cravath four games to one. Alex had the first of three consecutive 30-win seasons and Cactus had twenty-four homers as the National League's top home-run producer. Still, they were no match for Boston and its marvelous pitchers: Ernie Shore, Joe Wood, Rube Foster, and Hub Leonard. (Young Babe Ruth was quite a pitcher, too, but Carrigan didn't use him in the 1915 Series.)

The Federal League died after the 1915 season yet managed to bluff the majors into a handsome settlement. Sinclair having moved the Indianapolis Hoosiers, the 1914 champs, to Newark, now threatened to shift the team to New York in 1916. The majors had had enough. They sued for peace and it cost them. They had to pay a huge indemnity, agree to let the Fed owners in St. Louis and Chicago buy the Browns and the Cubs, and repurchase their jumpers from a players' pool. Outfielder Benny Kauff, the Feds' leading hitter both years, appeared to be the prize catch. The Giants paid $30,000 for him, but he never lived up to his promise. The best of the bunch proved to be Edd Roush, a fine outfielder and a strong-minded man with a keen sense of his own value. He held out most of 1922 in a salary dispute with the Reds and did not play at all in 1930, when he could not come to terms with McGraw. He batted .323 for the eighteen years that people paid him what he thought he deserved.

The Red Sox sold Speaker to Cleveland in 1916, rather than pay him what he wanted. It seemed the height of folly, even though the Sox won the pennant and World Series again. Speaker was Joe Wood's roommate, a

Hub favorite, and obviously one of the all-time greats. As though to prove the point, Spoke batted a spectacular .386 for the Indians to win the American League hitting crown. Ty Cobb was second with .371—the only year between 1907 and 1919 that he was not the league's top hitter. Cobb's records are so awesome that it is difficult to comprehend them. Twelve batting titles are phenomenal. Only another giant, Wagner, is even within striking distance: eight in twelve years. (Or Hornsby, seven in nine.) In this thirteen-year stretch Cobb averaged .378, a figure Foxx, Musial, Mays, Mantle, and Aaron never achieved even once in their distinguished careers. He was unarguably the dominant baseball presence of his time. But his greatness was singular.

He was a furious, smoldering, rancorous man. His desire to excel was a torment. It seems almost to have made him a bit crazy. For all his greatness he was friendly with no one. All hot-blooded competitors fought the foe, as McGraw fought the Cubs and Pirates and Cardinals. But for Cobb the enemy was everywhere. He had painful relationships with his teammates, he leaped into the stands to battle fans, he was an intolerant perfectionist and a failure as a manager. *My Life in Baseball*, Al Stump's brilliantly elicited autobiography of Cobb based on interviews in the last year of his life, is an astounding testament. The troubled past lived on in the old outfielder's mind, hurting like a wound in bad weather. Every facet was reexamined, explained, denied, justified, reinterpreted, and occasionally regretted. He sounded as though he wished he'd been a kinder, more likable, and thus more popular man, though on reflection, calculating how much of the essential Cobb he would have had to surrender, he seemed to find the cost too great. They should have loved him as he was.

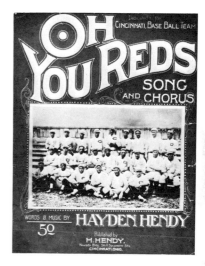

Impossible. He was admired and respected, though mostly people seem to have been fascinated by him—by his speed, his craft, his opportunism, his daring, and his fiery perfection, and also by watching his short fuse burn and wondering how he was going to explode. James T. Farrell, who has the era clearly in mind, remembers that when the Tigers were in town fans would say, "I think I'll go out to the ball park and see what Ty will do."

For twenty-four years he played baseball wonderfully well, even drilling three hits in a rain-shortened doubleheader against the Yankees in 1928, the first pro ball games one fan ever saw. Ty was forty-one then, playing for the Athletics in his last year, but he hit .323 for the season, and there was never any doubt, when he stood at the plate in the wide pants and three-quarter sleeves of those old A's uniforms, that he knew exactly what to do with the bat. The right hand held the handle an inch from the end, the left was placed a hand's breadth away. It was a control hitter's grip, the left hand serving as the fulcrum of a lever when bat met ball. But don't forget, those hands could slide together for power when the occasion demanded. One hit that day was a double. The Yankee pitcher, George Pipgras, wound up, kicked a leg, and threw. The bat came round in a level swing and the ball took flight. Memory doesn't say who handled it, but in the movies behind the eye Ty still makes the turn, digs for second, and slides in easily under Tony Lazzeri. It was one of more than four thousand hits. Perhaps the saddest commentary on Ty Cobb is that no major leaguer coming after him has ever tried to copy the batting style of the greatest hitter of all time.

Team was honored in song, but victory was forever tainted.

57

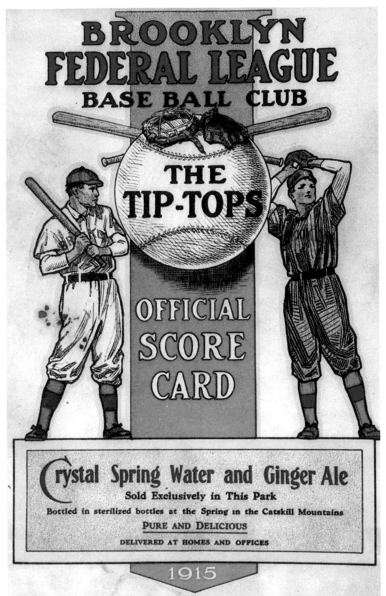

*Mementos of Federal
League's two years of
existence,* right *and*
above. *League had
too few stars to survive.*
Opposite bottom:
*Chicago Whales finished
second and first.*
Opposite top: *Red Sox, now
minus Speaker, whipped
Phils in 1915 Series.
Ruth won 18 during season
but was not needed
to pitch in Series.*

The year 1917 began a cycle of triumph and tragedy for the White
Sox. A team of no particular distinction since the Hitless Wonders of glorious
memory, it finally found a winning combination once more.

Right-hander Jim Scott and outfielder Shano Collins had been
with the Sox for several years. Buck Weaver, the dimpled third baseman with
the powerful bat, came up from Portland, in the young Pacific Coast League,
in 1912. Eddie Cicotte, master of the shine ball, was acquired from Boston
in midseason. Milwaukee provided Ray Schalk in 1913 for $18,000 and
Happy Felsch in 1915 for $12,000. Schalk wasn't big enough to swat flies, but
he could catch better than 120 games a season, and Happy was one of the
finest defensive outfielders in either league. Red Faber, who never played for
anyone but the Sox (like Ted Lyons) showed up in 1914; what a marvel he
was. Eddie Collins was bought at the end of the year. Joe Jackson and Nemo
Leibold, who shared right field with Shano, were bought from Cleveland, an-

The players appear as follows, reading from left to right: Standing - Collins, Wood, Gainer, Shore, Barry, Ruth, Mays, Hoblitzel, Dr. Green [Trainer]. Sitting - Leonard, Henriksen, Gardner, Carrigan [Manager], Cady, Janvrin, Thomas. On ground - Lewis, Wagner, McNally, Hooper, Cooper and Scott

No. 260

RED SOX READY TO DO BATTLE FOR WORLD'S CHAMPIONSHIP

CHICAGO 1915 WHALES
FEDERAL LEAGUE CHAMPIONS

1. Farrel, 2b.
2. Wagner, c.
3. Johnson, p.
4. Tinker, s.s.
5. Weeghman, Pres.
6. Beck, 1b.
7. Black, p.
8. Clemons, c.
9. Jackson, 1b.
10. Mann, o.f.
11. Hendrix, p.
12. Smith, s.s.
13. Lang, p.
14. Brennan, p.
15. Wickland, o.f.
16. Fischer, c.
17. Wilson, c.
18. Zwilling, o.f.
19. Prendergast, p.
20. Hanford, o.f.
21. Flack, o.f.
22. Kavanagh, o.f.
23. McConnell, p.
24. Brown, p.

59

Top: *1914 Miracle Braves—key players were, from left, front row: Joe Connolly (1) Dick Rudolph (4), Maranville (5), Evers (8); middle: Lefty Tyler (3); top: Bill James (1), Hank Gowdy (9), Butch Schmidt (10). Above: Roger Bresnahan (center) in spring training pepper game, 1915.*

other club in financial straits, in mid-1915. Jackson cost $31,500. Claud Williams and Dave Danforth, two lefties, and infielder Fred McMullin arrived in 1916. Chick Gandil, another purchase from the Indians, gave them the experienced first baseman they needed, and hard-eyed, close-mouthed Swede Risberg took over at short, both in 1917. Curiously, Charlie Comiskey, whose niggardly salaries have always been blamed for nudging the Black Sox toward crime, was considered the last of the big spenders and criticized for trying to buy a pennant with his outlays of cash.

Well, who doesn't? Certainly he bought wisely. When baseball's all-time top teams are under discussion this one is always mentioned. They beat the Red Sox by nine and met a transitional Giant team in the Series. There were few faces from McGraw's last winner, in 1913, and few who would be around for his next, in 1921. The Sox won a good Series as Faber took three games and Cicotte one.

The Red Sox came back to take the pennant in 1918, but by mid-summer the reality of war had begun to bite. More than two hundred ballplayers had entered the armed forces, the season ground to a halt after 129 games, and the World Series was held only by special dispensation from Washington—the Government, not Clark Griffith. With Ruth and Mays each winning a pair, the Red Sox took the Cubs. It was Boston's last hurrah.

The White Sox repeated in 1919, and Cincinnati surprised by finishing on top in the National. Cicotte won twenty-nine, Williams twenty-three. Jackson's Black Betsy hit for a .351 average. On defense Felsch had the remarkable total of thirty-two outfield assists and Leibold twenty-six. Faber, a victim of the flu epidemic, was under par all year. Young Dickie Kerr stepped in to win thirteen. A fine season. The Sox were favored and there seemed no doubt they would take the Series easily.

How and why they didn't is baseball's most bizarre episode, as fascinating as it was shameful because the full story will never be known. Games certainly were thrown; Cicotte and Williams's confessions of deliberate bad pitching established that. Gandil set the scheme in motion. Felsch and Jackson took money. Risberg, Weaver, and McMullin knew what was going on. Yet ambiguity remains. Jackson got twelve hits and batted .375; Weaver batted .324; both played errorless ball. Gandil decided both of honest Dickie Kerr's two wins with timely hits. McMullin got one pinch hit in two at-bats, his total performance in the Series, so how could he cheat? Ironically, the Clean Sox, except for Kerr, were unimpressive. Eddie Collins hit .226 and made two errors. Shano and Nemo had five hits in thirty-four at-bats between them.

There was more to know, but those who might have enlightened us never did, not the culprits, not the teammates who played it straight, not the club and league officials or their network of lawyers. Mum was the word.

It was a sad time for the Reds, whose victory lost its luster. They were a better team than people thought. They won their pennant by nine games (the Sox beat Cleveland by three and a half), they had top hitters in Edd Roush and Heinie Groh, they had good pitching from Hod Eller, Dutch Reuther, and Slim Sallee. Who can say they wouldn't have won even with the White Sox on the level?

Owner Charles Ebbets, the Squire of Flatbush, and daughter Miss Genevieve at Dodger opening game.

Opposite top: *1919 White Sox two weeks before infamous Series began. From left top: manager Gleason (1), Risberg (5), McMullin (6); middle: Schalk (1), Kerr (4), Felsch (5), Gandil (6), Weaver (7); bottom: Eddie Collins (1), Cicotte (3).* Opposite bottom right: *Joe Jackson hit .375 but shared spoils.* Opposite bottom left: *29-game winner Cicotte threw two games.* Left: *Pat Moran on Cincinnati program for 1919.* Above: *Ten key Reds.*

Chapter 4

THE SULTAN OF SWAT

1920-1932

Babe Ruth happened to baseball at just the right time and he was exactly the right thing to have happened. In 1920 the game was depleted by the war, stultified by internal quarrels, and tarnished by the Black Sox scandal, a story that was leaking like poison gas. Baseball needed nothing so much as a breath of fresh air and a return to the simple American virtues it liked to believe it had always represented. Babe, with his big bat, his raw energy, and his arms-wide welcome to life, worked a magic change in baseball's atmosphere and image.

Like all human beings he was a complicated man, although what was up front, for all to see, was easy to understand and easy to like. He was large in every way—in body, in appetites, in talent. He was good with kids, fun to be around, and got a kick out of the game he played so well. Once those home runs started clearing the fences of every park in the American League, he was a cynosure and everyone's hero.

There were two Babes, of course: the youthful lefty who pitched for the Red Sox and the home-run king of the Yankees. Babe was proud of the youngster and never forgot his achievements. In six seasons, the last two of which he also played the outfield, he won eighty-nine and lost forty-six, an impressive .659 percentage. One season he had nine shutouts, beat Walter Johnson four times, and had the league's best ERA. Another year he led in home runs, then pitched two winning World Series games. His twenty-nine and two-thirds scoreless innings pitched over two Series were a record until Whitey Ford spun thirty-two in 1960 and 1961, a decade after Babe's death.

But everyone liked the home-run hitter better, and no one lamented the passing of the pitching star. However good he was, Ruth the pitcher was no novelty, whereas Ruth the hitter was phenomenal. In the course of those 714 home runs (49 for the Red Sox, 659 for the Yankees, and 6, at the end, for the Braves) in 2,503 games over twenty-two years, fans, teammates, even opponents never tired of the power and artistry of his swing. His most incredible statistic is the one that has never really been approached and is unlikely to be surpassed: one home run every 11.76 times at bat. None of the heaviest sluggers of baseball history—not Gehrig, Foxx, Mays, Mantle, not Ott, Frank Robinson, Mathews, Aaron—has come close to it. (Second is Ralph Kiner, 14.11, then Harmon Killebrew, Willie McCovey, and Ted Williams.) Nor is anyone close to his lifetime slugging average of .690.

Everyone who saw him undoubtedly has a particular memory, for he was legitimately, genuinely heroic; all the hyperbole was true. The memorable hit on May 21, 1932, came in the first game of a doubleheader with the Senators at Yankee Stadium. Washington had a pretty good team that year and was bucking the Yanks for first place. But as has happened so often to non-New York teams in American League pennant races in the past half-century, the Yankees broke their hearts.

Two lefties pitched the opener: Lloyd Brown against Herb Pennock. Brown wasn't bad, but Pennock was a master, pitching with his accustomed ease and finesse. He seemed easy to hit. He never was overpowering. He struck out few and walked fewer, so everyone swung and got wood on the ball but to no avail. There were rollers to the infield, lazy flies to the outfield. This game the Senators managed to score a couple early and were

How Babe swung the bat: Grasp pages 63 through 109 at edge above this caption and riffle them rapidly. Flip-card action will show you a "movie" of Ruth's inimitable big swing.

Here begins "flipbook" section of the Babe Ruth swing.

65

Babe's enormous impact was seen in array of products trading on his name. Top: Still from Ruthian movie, *above:* Bambino brand tobacco.

leading 2-1 as the Yanks came to bat in the fifth. Pennock, no hitter, singled—an ill omen for Washington. Earle Combs, the lead-off man, hit a double-play grounder to Myer at second and Buddy muffed it. Everybody safe. The full-house crowd of some sixty thousand began a hollow, hungry roar of anticipation. It was clear that if Lyn Lary got on, Babe would come to bat with the bases full. Brown pitched too carefully, probably trying to keep the ball low in hopes of a double play. Lary walked. Oh, those bases on balls!

The crowd noise rose to a high, exultant pitch. Only one resolution seemed possible, or acceptable. Babe did not prolong the drama. He tippytoed to the plate and whacked Brown's first pitch into the right-field stands.

He owned that right field. It was short: 296 feet and with only a low field-box railing as the final barrier. Many of his high-arcing mortar shots—like this one—dropped in there. Ruth was a belter, too, however. When he didn't pull them, they were just as likely to go into the Yankee bull pen, or the right-center bleachers, or, in other cities, right out of the park.

Gehrig followed him with a double. Ben Chapman singled Lou to third and stole second. Lazzeri socked another home run. A seven-run inning. There was no fight in the Senators after that.

If you didn't like the Yankees it was a tough time to be alive.

The Ruthian Age began as World War I ended. The survivors laughed with relief and plunged into a wave of postwar prosperity, a time of high jinks, bootleg booze, and a bull market, of automobiles, radios, and airplanes, of Jazz Age flappers, Hollywood stars, and sports champions.

For the big leagues it was a lively era with a lively ball. Reach and Spalding, the manufacturers, said they were using a strong Australian wool yarn that wound tighter and gave the ball more zip. Pitchers said that if you held one to your ear you could hear the rabbit's heart beating.

The majors also outlawed those freak deliveries that had contributed so much to pitchers' supremacy. Henceforth, there was to be no tampering with the ball, no burdening it with foreign substances, such as spit.

In midseason one of Carl Mays's submarine balls (an up-from-under fastball) struck the Indians' shortstop, Ray Chapman, in the head and killed him. Mays was a dour fellow and Ray habitually crowded the plate, but no one ever suggested it was a beanball. Chapman either didn't see it or froze. Shocked at its first fatal accident on the field, the majors immediately ordered more new balls into play, so batters could see them more clearly, so there would be less chance of a ball being scuffed and flying out of control.

This combination of factors dramatically altered the balance of the game. There was a noticeable increasé in .300 hitters and home runs. Ruth leaped to an incredible total of fifty-four, nearly twice as many as had ever been hit before. He caused tremendous excitement. The Yankees' attendance doubled and "the Bambino"—"the Sultan of Swat," "the King of Clout"—became baseball's greatest drawing card on the road, as well. Curiosity about how many runs he had been responsible for in 1919 began the calculation of runs batted in, which soon became one of the game's fundamental statistics.

Cleveland, with young Joe Sewell replacing Chapman, won the pennant in a tight race with the White Sox and Yankees. (The Black Sox

played the season. Their infamous, badly kept secret hit the headlines in late September: "Bare Fixed World Series.") The unobtrusive Sewell became a first-rate fielder and a steady hitter who was almost impossible to strike out. In 7,976 at-bats over fourteen years (counting bases on balls), he fanned just 114 times—once every seventy trips to the plate.

Brooklyn won in the National League, Robby's Robins playing the famous, twenty-six inning, 1-1 tie with Boston en route. The Giants were second and the Reds made third after playing the Pirates three games in one day to decide the final standing.

It was another best-of-nine Series and the Indians won easily, aided in game five by such first-ever oddities as an unassisted triple play (Bill Wambsganss), a grand-slam homer (Elmer Smith), and a pitcher's four-bagger (Jim Bagby). Brooklyn's Clarence Mitchell, who hit into the triple play, hit into a double play his next time up: five outs in two at-bats.

In 1921 the Yankee dynasty was founded and the first of more than thirty pennants won. Harry Frazee, pressed for cash to complete his purchase of the Red Sox, found a ready market in New York for his stars. By 1923 twelve players would be shipped to the Yankees. Aside from Ruth, there were a regular catcher, shortstop, and third baseman, and five first-line pitchers. It was a scandal, but the new high commissioner of baseball, Kenesaw Mountain Landis, evidently did not think it altered significantly the competitive balance of the American League. In any event he took no action.

Colonel Ruppert also was shrewd enough to pluck Ed Barrow from the Red Sox dugout and install him in the Yankee front office as business manager. Excellence on the field was already assured. Miller Huggins was starting a tradition of managerial excellence. Barrow promised excellence in the executive suite. He completed ransacking the Red Sox and kept his new employers champions for a generation.

The Yanks' sudden prominence was a direct challenge to McGraw's supremacy in New York, the more so since both clubs played at the Polo Grounds while Yankee Stadium was rising across the river. The landlord beat the tenant in two Series under Coogan's Bluff, but in 1923, capping their first season in "the House That Ruth Built," the Yanks beat McGraw for their first world championship.

Everything about baseball was getting bigger in the twenties. Seventy percent of the nation's growing population lived east of the Mississippi, as did the major leagues (except for St. Louis). Attendance was up fifty percent from the previous decade. Part of the boost came from the crowds at weekend doubleheaders as the "blue laws" that had prohibited Sunday ball for nearly fifty years were overturned. And part probably resulted from the game's increasing popularity through radio broadcasts. The Series was aired by relay in 1921; by 1925 the Cubs were permitting the first daily broadcasts of home games.

If times were changing, the twenties still had clubs that lived familiarly among their fans. Brooklyn always springs to mind, but there were others: Boston, Cincinnati, St. Louis, Cleveland. The parks were small and often on irregularly shaped plots. Homes and apartments crowded close around them. They were as much a part of the neighborhood as the firehouse,

This cheap watch runs today. Yankee fan who owns it always takes it to Stadium as good-luck charm.

the tavern, or the bakery. Admissions had increased little. Bleachers were 55¢, the grandstand $1.10, and a box seat $1.65. Kids could get in free by working a turnstile or helping sweep trash from the stands. Once inside you were pleasantly close to the field. You could see the expression on a player's face, exchange a few words or a wave with an outfielder as he took his position near your part of the bleachers, hear the home team's cries of encouragement and its ragging of the opposition. Owners such as Charley Ebbets, "the Squire of Flatbush," held court in the stands, listening to profound strategies and suggestions for trades, or simply bantering with folks who had been there the day before and would come out tomorrow.

A number of clubs were less than thriving. The Braves, Red Sox, and Phillies were hopeless have-nots, always in seventh or eighth place. The White Sox, destroyed by the loss of the eight men out, floundered in the second division, although three times the excellent Ted Lyons won more than twenty games for them. Brooklyn, ridiculously, had a lock on sixth place: seven times in eight years. Still, the skies seemed bright and, as the Phils' manager, Burt Shotton, was fond of saying (his voice rising hollowly from the National League cellar): "Time is a great leveler in baseball."

The Athletics and Cardinals would have agreed with him. Step by step, Connie Mack was moving his team back up the ladder. By 1927 he was in second place, almost there. Already aboard were Al Simmons, the only foot-in-the-bucket hitter with a .334 lifetime average; Lefty Grove, a 300-game winner; Gordon ("Mickey") Cochrane, regarded everywhere but in Bill Dickey country as the best catcher of the modern era; and Jimmie Foxx, who came within two of Ruth's home-run record. George Earnshaw and Mule Haas were the only important players still to come.

As for the Cardinals, they were becoming competitive on the strength of Branch Rickey's unique farm system. A brilliant conception by one of the game's few creative intelligences (whom John Kieran of the *Times* always called Branch, the Non-Alcoholic Rickey), it was the perfect way for a poor club with a small park and a penurious owner to stay even with the big guys. The system had not yet come into full flower, but by ownership or control of clubs at every level of the minor leagues, and by an army of players under contract, it assured St. Louis of excellent, inexpensive replacements for a steadily improving team.

The big team of the decade, and possibly of all time, was the 1927 Yankees. They won 110 games—a .714 pace—and left the second-place Athletics eating their dust, 19 games behind. They blasted every pitcher in sight. No one could hold them. They had a team batting average of .307. Gehrig hit .373, Ruth and Combs .356, Bob Meusel .337, and Lazzeri .309. Ruth's sixty homers were historic. They were nearly fourteen percent of the homers hit in the league that year and more than the totals hit by twelve of the majors' sixteen teams. Gehrig's forty-seven also were pretty impressive and he had 175 RBIs, as well, the most ever to that time.

Other teams have had superlative seasons, of course. What made 1927 the Yankee year was the team's aptness as a symbol of the times. They were proficient and overwhelmingly successful, and made it look easy. Which was about the way Americans regarded themselves as the boom

roared on, seemingly without effort, showering the benefits of the economy across the land, and with no end in sight.

The Yankees moved serenely into the World Series, facing Pittsburgh, a strong team. Pie Traynor was surely the best third baseman around. He was a superb fielder, a hitter strong enough to bat clean-up, and a gent—the Brooks Robinson of his time, but with a better bat. The Waner family supplied two-thirds of the outfield—Paul and Lloyd—left-handed batters with eagle eyes and amazing control. They were greyhounds, slender and fast, with flat swings that sprayed singles and doubles all over the field, though perhaps most often on a line over second. Lloyd led off; in this, his freshman year, he hit .355. Paul, hitting second, topped the league at .380.

The story persists that, good as they were, the Pirates were psyched before a pitch was thrown. They watched the Yankees' Murderers' Row smash ball after ball into the seats in a pre-Series workout and went into shock. True or not, they blew the Series in four straight. The Yanks then took four in a row from the 1928 Cardinals (Babe went ten for sixteen, a .625 average) and four in a row from the 1932 Cubs.

These Yankees set the style for generations to come. They already had the businesslike pin-stripe uniform (in 1929 they added identifying numbers, the first club of modern times to do so) and the businesslike manner on the field. Babe was flamboyant in all he did, yet however much he caroused after hours, his demeanor was thoroughly professional during a game. The Yanks were good and they knew it.

Curiously, though, the 1927 Yankees were better than the sum of their parts, and actually they did not play together very long as a unit. Shortstop Mark Koenig was in the third of five-plus years, an able fellow but no match for Frank Crosetti or Phil Rizzuto. "Jumping Joe" Dugan had lost much of his bounce and was in his last year. (Willie Kamm of the White Sox and Ossie Bluege of the Senators were far superior third basemen.) This was the last good year for Bob Meusel, the rifle-armed outfielder. Dutch Reuther, who pitched for the 1919 Reds, was about done. Urban Shocker, an accomplished pitcher, was fatally ill and died in 1928. And surprising Wilcy Moore, the jolly farmer who won nineteen games, mostly in relief, never found the touch again. Finally, no great team ever had such inferior catching. Benny Bengough, Pat Collins, Johnny Grabowski—they couldn't hit, they were only moderately good defensively, and none of them could catch more than half a season. The heart of the team was Ruth, Gehrig, Combs, Lazzeri, plus Hoyt, Pennock, and Pipgras—a strong heart, but could they have been the greatest of all time?

By the late twenties hitters had driven the pitchers to cover. It was a startling turnabout and had taken place in less than ten years. Most of the weapons of the previous decade were rusting from disuse. The bunt, the sacrifice, the stolen base—who needed them? Games weren't decided by one run any more.

The hitting *was* fearsome. Babe got 467 of his homers in this decade. Rogers Hornsby had a five-year span in which he averaged .402, including a fantastic .424 in 1924. The nine .300 hitters of 1915 became thirty-five by 1927, seventy-one by 1929, and eighty-seven in 1930, the peak year. The

More memorabilia of Sultan of Swat—right: American League ball bears famous signature; above: belt buckles, common emblems, usually signified membership in one Babe Ruth club or another. Opposite: Front and back of Babe's monthly check in 1922—a huge sum at the time.

four .400 hitters between 1900 and 1920 (two of them Cobb) became eight in the decade to 1930.

In 1930 the Giants had the highest team average of all time: .319. Every team in the National League, except Cincinnati and Boston, hit .300 or better, as did three in the American. The Phils hit .315, but their pitchers allowed 1,199 runs, a horrible 7.8 per game, and they finished eighth. (No surprise. In the twenty-seven years between 1919 and 1945, they were seventh or eighth twenty-four times.) Bill Terry hit .401; no one in the National League has topped him since. Hack Wilson had 56 homers and 190 RBIs, still the major league record. The majors hit 1,565 homers.

The Nationals took a little dynamite out of the ball a year later and averages promptly slumped. Chick Hafey eked out the batting crown in what was nearly a triple dead heat: .3489 to Terry's .3486 and "Sunny Jim" Bottomley's .3482. The American League gave the rabbit another year of life.

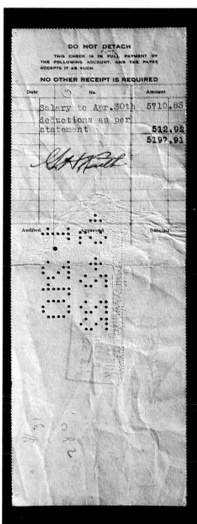

Connie Mack completed the climb from the basement in 1929, with another championship team, mowing down the Yankees after three years of close pursuit. Shrewd old Connie—he was already sixty-seven—astonished everyone by starting veteran right-hander Howard Ehmke against the Cubs in the first game of the Series. He had decided that his lefties—even Grove—would be eaten alive by the fastball hitters of the Cubs' predominantly right-handed lineup. Unawed by the awesome Cuyler, Wilson, Hornsby, Stephenson and Charlie Grimm, good gray Howard fanned thirteen and won 3-1. The cruncher, of course, was the famous fourth game, in which the A's, losing 8-0, sent fifteen men to bat in the seventh and scored ten game-winning runs.

The Series ended only days before the Crash, the sudden, sickening plunge of stock-market prices that exposed the economic malaise underlying the Boom. The giddy success of the twenties lost its momentum and the nation was pitched into the harrowing years of the Depression.

The Athletics repeated in 1930—"the Year of the Bat"—and 1931,

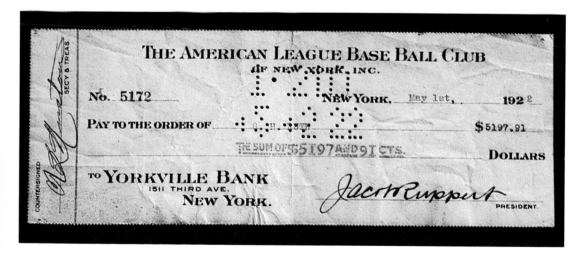

Top: *Young Gehrig belts one (in print from broken glass-plate negative). Facing Lou after the Babe was a trial for pitchers.* Above: *Yankees of 1927 are among the greatest all-time teams; it can even be argued that they were the greatest. Among their challengers would have to be Joe McCarthy's Yankees and Casey Stengel's.*

both times facing the Cardinals in the Series. The 1930 Cardinals were another power-hitting team. Eight regulars had better-than-.300 averages. But the A's could hit a bit, too; their pitchers were superb, and they won.

The 1931 rematch saw the Athletics at their peak. Irascible Lefty Grove ("Robert," Connie called him, or "Groves") put together the kind of season that hadn't been seen since the old days: 31-4, an .886 percentage. He was as near to invincible as a pitcher can be. He won two games in the Series, as well, but they weren't enough. The man who made the difference was a newcomer to the Cardinal lineup—Pepper Martin, a hatchet-faced young outfielder who was the archetypal Cardinal farmhand: lean, unpolished, aggressive, and a winner. As is well remembered, for it has become one of baseball's epic stories, Pepper demolished the A's almost by himself. He batted .500, rapping twelve hits, four of them doubles, one a homer. He scored five runs, batted in five, and personally accounted for two of the Cardinal victories. On the bases he was a terror, embarrassing the excellent Mickey Cochrane with five stolen bases—ungraceful, hell-for-leather sprints and head-first slides that earned him the nickname "Wild Horse of the Osage."

The Yankees, stunned by the death of Miller Huggins as the 1929 season ended, found themselves a new manager in Joseph V. McCarthy, who had handled the Cubs with fair success since 1926. He had lost his one Series unhandsomely to the Athletics, but the Yanks saw him as their kind of man.

Joe produced. In the next thirteen years he never finished lower than third and that only once. He won eight pennants and seven World Series, in which the opposition took a total of five games.

"Marse Joe" was never given to sentiment, yet he probably never enjoyed any Series more than his first, when the 1932 Yankees blanked the Cubs, four-zip. The Yanks scored thirty-seven runs on forty-five hits. Not one game was close. One, however, produced the most famous home run in World Series history: Babe Ruth's shot off Charley Root at Wrigley Field in the fifth inning of the third game.

Did he call it? Did he take two strikes, waggling fingers at the Cub bench to acknowledge the count, then point to the center field bleachers and sock the longest home run ever seen at Wrigley Field right to the spot?

Some newspaper accounts said he did, and thus a legend was born. Others, oddly, failed to mention it. Players on the field that day deny that it happened. Root, a tough competitor, protested until the day he died that he would have knocked Ruth on his butt with a fastball under the chin rather than let him try to make good on such an audacious gesture. Ruth himself never tried to clarify the confusion. Why ruin one of the fabulous sports stories of all time?

The fact remains that the Cubs were riding the Bambino hard. The bench jockeying was savage. The crowd was hostile and jeering. And the Babe was enjoying the tumult. Although the score was tied, the Cubs were being clobbered. Ruth had already hit a three-run homer off Root in the first. He was the Yankees' big man and the target of the Cubs' frustration and despair. What better moment to acknowledge each called strike, then bend to the business at hand and park one in the seats? The only conceivably more magnificent gesture would have been to point to the spot beforehand.

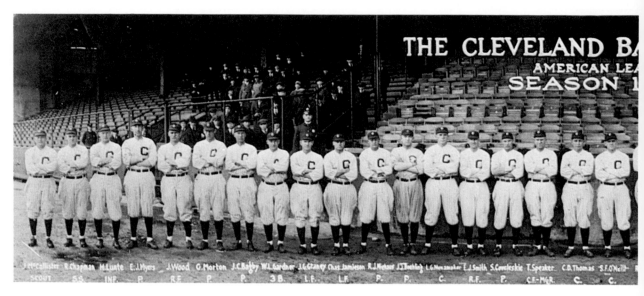

Top: *Tris Speaker's champion Indians of 1920.* Above right:
*Enamel pins for press or other favored folks are old tradition
in baseball. Stadium pin was for first game in House That Ruth
Built.* Above left: *Commemorative matchbox was Ty Cobb's.* Opposite
left: *Willie Kamm had solid career for White Sox and Indians.
Here he plays for San Francisco Seals a year before his purchase
by Chicago.* Opposite right: *Ticket for Game 3 of 1923
Series. Stengel homer won it 1-0 for Giants over Yanks.*

ZEENUT
SERIES
1922
KAMM
S.F

Stars of the 1920s.
Above: Waite Hoyt
at start of fine
pitching career
with Yankees. Right:
Cards from W-502-
503 series are
prominent National
Leaguers. Opposite:
Giants' Fred Lindstrom,
left, and Casey Stengel,
and scene of game at
Polo Grounds in
1920. Fly ball has been
hit to right with
runners on first and
third. Note: There
are only two umpires
and playing field
is in poor condition.

76

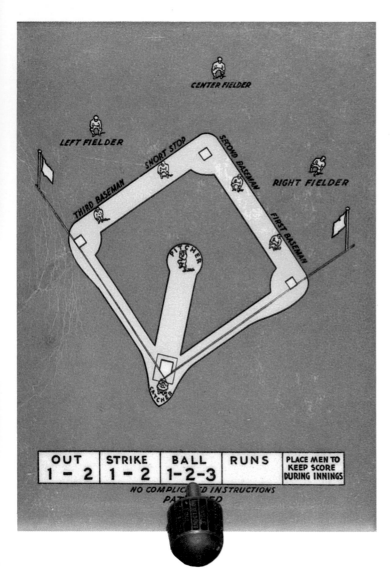

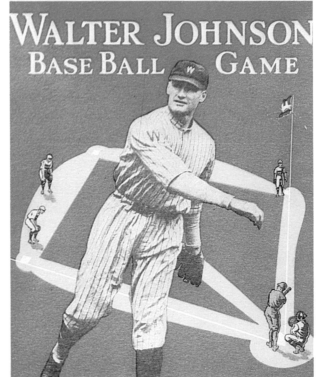

Opposite, clockwise from top: *Crack-a-Jack uniforms offer six swatches of flannel. Johnson may or not have worn the product, but manufacturer would have welcomed any inference that his uniforms matched the quality and integrity of the Big Train. Medal from Senators' win over Giants. Bad hop decided it. In 1925 Deacon Bill's Pirates won in seven as Johnson's career neared end.* Above: *Black spinner (at bottom of field) marked game's progress.*

Baseball
Uniforms
Made to
Order

Johnson — of the Senators

These Baseball Uniform Samples show you the weave, the texture, and the quality of the different grades of cloth.

Measure Taking and Prices

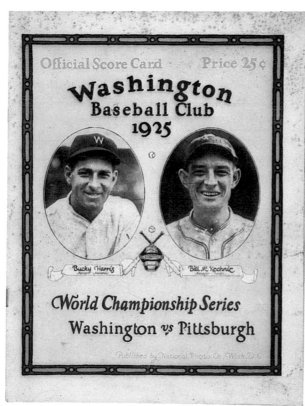

Official Score Card · Price 25¢

Washington
Baseball Club
1925

Bucky Harris

Bill McKechnie

World Championship Series

Washington vs Pittsburgh

Published by National Photo Co., Wash. D.C.

Above: *Autographed photo of 1925
Washington club, which won
second flag under boy manager
Bucky Harris. Dutch Reuther
of 1919 Reds is fifth from left in
rear. Tom Zachary, fated to
give up Babe's sixtieth homer
in 1927, is ninth. Find Walter
Johnson, Goose Goslin, Sam Rice,
Muddy Ruel.* Right: *Two phases
of Grover Alexander's career:
the Phils' ace who averaged
27 wins for seven years
and Cards' old hero (minus
cardboard glove hand) winding
down in his forties.* Opposite:
*Harry Heilmann had big
years in Detroit outfield with
Cobb, won American League batting
crown, oddly, in odd-numbered
years: 1921, 1923, 1925, 1927.*

Right: *Happy slugger was Cards' first baseman Sunny Jim Bottomley. A lifetime .310 hitter, he had 12 RBIs (on six hits) in nine innings against Dodgers in 1924. He also was third in near-triple dead heat for National League batting crown in 1931.* Opposite top: *Al Simmons, A's strong left fielder, was honored with ten-cent cigar in his home town.* Opposite bottom: *Shirt of Bill Wambsganss, famous for unassisted triple play in 1920 World Series. He finished up as utility man for Connie Mack. Rampant white elephant was familiar Athletics' symbol.*

JIM BOTTOMLEY
N.L.most valuable player 1928
"Toasting gives a flavor no other cigarette can equal"

Opposite: *Contributing mightily to heavy hitting of 1929 Phils were Chuck Klein (left) and Lefty O'Doul, who topped league at .398. Left: Well-traveled Burleigh Grimes won 270 games throwing spitballs for Pirates, Dodgers, Giants, Braves, Cards, Cubs, and Yanks. Below: 1927 Pirates had Paul Waner (seated left), Lloyd (2nd from right). Bottle-bat Heinie Groh is 4th from left in middle, Pie Traynor 7th. Three who did better elsewhere were Kiki Cuyler (4th from right rear), Joe Cronin (3rd), Dick Bartell (far right).*

Opposite top right and bottom: *Cards led by Deacon Bill were walloped by Yankees in 1928 Series. Opposite top left: Quartet of 1928 Reds had nothing to smile about. Reds' 1929 club finished seventh, heading for cellar. Red Lucas was ace of staff, Horace Ford played short, "Pid" Purdy outfield, Pinky Pittenger infield. Cards cost 5¢, were dispensed by slot machine. Left: D & M catalog. Bob O'Farrell was a fine catcher, Schulte is Cubs' "Wildfire," George Burns is Indians' first baseman, not National League outfielder of same name. Roger Peckinpaugh, excellent shortstop, made eight errors in 1925 Series for the Washington Senators.*

1929 Cubs enjoyed tremendous batting. *Hornsby*, left, *hit a big .380; Riggs Stephenson,* below, *.362; Hack Wilson,* opposite right, *.345. In 1930 Hack got 56 homers and set major league record of 190 RBIs.* Opposite top left: *Charley Root won 19. (Note simple lacing of glove.)* Opposite bottom left: *Manager Joe McCarthy was in Yankee dugout the next year.*

OFFICIAL *souvenir* PROGRAM

ST. LOUIS vs PHILADELPHIA
for the Championship of the World
SPORTSMAN'S PARK ~ 1931

SPIRIT OF ST. LOUIS

Connie Mack's last pennant-winning teams were Athletics of 1929-31. Bottom: 1929 array, which downed Cubs in five games. Eddie Collins and his manager on 1919 White Sox, Kid Gleason, are far left. Only nonsigner is Howard Ehmke, who fanned 13 Cubs in Series opener. Left: Swirl of stars won 1930 tilt with Cards but lost repeat in 1931. Opposite right: St. Louis program has three talismans: statue of Saint, Lindy's plane, and Cardinals. Opposite left: Muscular slugger, Jimmie Foxx.

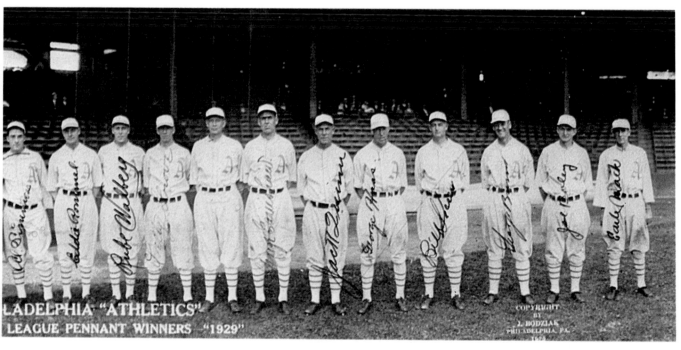

PHILADELPHIA "ATHLETICS"
LEAGUE PENNANT WINNERS "1929"

Above: *Pepper Martin wears a winner's grin. Aggressive and opportunistic, he played third and outfield with abandon for thirteen years.* Right: *Dazzy Vance was Dodger ace of 1920s, Babe Herman,* opposite, *a hard-hitting outfielder with partially deserved reputation for bizarre fielding. He also took part in Brooklyn's famous three-men-on-third baserunning fiasco.*

ARTHUR (DIZZY) VANCE

CHICAGO

HAZEN (KI-KI) CUYLER
CHICAGO

PAUL WANER

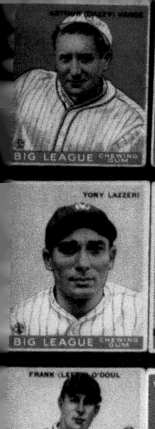
TONY LAZZERI

GUS MANCUSO

FRANK FRISCH

GEORGE HERMAN (BABE) RUTH

FRANK (LEFTY) O'DOUL

CHARLIE RUFFING

LOU GEHRIG

TRAVIS C. JACKSON

CHARLES (CHUCK) KLEIN

FRED FITZSIMMONS

OSWALD BLUEGE

LLOYD WANER

CHARLEY GEHRINGER

ROBERT (LEFTY) GROVE

LEWIS (HACK) WILSON

JEROME (DIZZY) DEAN

BIG LEAGUE CHEWING GUM

Goudey Big League series of 1933-34
came with slab of pink bubble
gum. Wax-paper wrapping was nearly opaque,
but kindly candy-store man would let
you thumb through box to avoid
purchase of duplicates. Cards were
redolent of sugar coating on gum for
years. Eventually there were 240 cards, but
by error #106 was omitted. Sharp-eyed
collectors who inquired were
given specially printed Lajoie card.

BASEBALL IN DEPRESSION AND WAR 1933-1945

The Depression exposed a fundamental and nearly fatal weakness of base-ball's structure. Traditionally a confederation of individual family enter-prises, the clubs proved to be grossly undercapitalized in the lean and strin-gent thirties. Clubs with small stadiums had limited revenues in the best of times. In straitened circumstances, with money tight and attendance falling off, many were hard-pressed to pay hotel and travel expenses, let alone the costs of farm operations, which the success of the Cardinals' chain gang was forcing on everyone. Only their monopoly position and their control of player salaries through the one-sided power of the reserve clause kept these quaint, paternalistic baronies open for business.

In the American League the lordly Yankees, the well-bankrolled Red Sox of Tom Yawkey, and the briefly successful Tigers of Walter Briggs breathed easily. In the National the Reds and Cubs, backed by radio and chewing-gum fortunes, and the Giants, backed by the loyalty and sentiment that winners accrue, did well. For everyone else it was hand-to-mouth.

The Phillies assured their noncompetitiveness by assiduously sell-ing off all players of quality to keep the franchise afloat. The best of these ex-Phils made a quite impressive team: Dolf Camilli, first base, Danny Mur-tagh, second base, Dick Bartell, shortstop, Pinky Whitney, third base, Chuck Klein, Lefty O'Doul, and Danny Litwhiler, outfield, Spud Davis, catcher, and Kirby Higbe, Curt Davis, Claude Passeau, and Bucky Walters, pitchers.

The Braves barely got by. In 1936 they became the Bees. It didn't help. Brooklyn had seriocomic legal and financial tangles that paralyzed the front office. Even the Cards, though rich in players, were short on cash. In the American League the franchises of three old players—Comiskey, Griffith, and Mack—were shoestring operations.

When he failed to win a fourth straight pennant in 1932, saintly Connie gutted his team once more. Again the excuse was hard times and lack of money, but it can't have been necessary to unload *everyone*. As in 1914, he made his first deal with the White Sox, sending them Al Simmons, Jimmy Dykes, and Mule Haas. The following year Mickey Cochrane was dealt to De-troit, where he promptly won two pennants as player-manager. Grove, Max Bishop, and Rube Walberg were dispatched to Boston, George Earnshaw to Chicago. A year later the Red Sox got Bing Miller and the year after that Jim-mie Foxx. They also got the two shortstops who succeeded Joe Boley. Age re-tired Howard Ehmke. Ed Rommel became an umpire. And interminable Jack Quinn departed Philadelphia to pitch capably in relief for Brooklyn at forty-seven. In four years no one was left from the pennant winners of 1931.

Mr. Mack got top dollar for his stars, and some interesting replace-ments were quickly acquired: Doc Cramer, Bob Johnson, Wally Moses, Pinky Higgins, and, for one season at any rate, Paul Rapier Richards, the thoughtful and unsmiling catcher from Waxahachie, Texas. There were some fine ca-reers in the making here. But no one replaced Cochrane's versatility or Foxx's enormous power, and the pitching was decimated. It can be argued that the staff Mack lost had few productive years left. Only Grove continued to win. Yet the replacements were worse. Never again in Mack's lifetime, never again in Philadelphia, would the A's have more than one good pitcher at a time. No manager in baseball history finished last as often as Connie Mack.

The dominant team in this period, as in others, was the Yankees: seven pennants and six world championships. Detroit had four pennants, Washington one, and the Browns their one and only. The National League was better balanced, as it always has been, with pennants scattered among five teams: Cards four (plus three world championships), Giants and Cubs three each, Cincinnati two, and the Dodgers, at the beginning of their rise to eminence, one.

It was also a period when a generation of old ballplayers, reaching the end of their playing days, began managerial careers of astonishing longevity. Their senior was "Deacon" Bill McKechnie, who began outfielding for the Pirates in 1907, first became a manager in the Federal League, and from 1928 to 1946 guided the Cards, Braves, and Reds. A patient, even-tempered man, he won the occasional pennant with good material, never disgraced himself with bad.

Another old outfielder, a well-regarded professional despite a capricious nature, was Casey Stengel, who showed no particular promise as manager of Brooklyn or of Boston in its incarnation as the Bees. His time would come.

Five were player-managers briefly before retiring to the bench: Jimmy Dykes, "the Little Round Man" of the White Sox; "Jolly Cholly" Grimm of the Cubs, a left-handed banjo player, raconteur, and one-time teammate and companion of the companionable Rabbit Maranville; Joe Cronin of Washington and the Red Sox; Leo Durocher of Brooklyn; and Bill Terry of the Giants. By the end of their time as players and managers they would aggregate 182 years of baseball experience.

There was also a long-term manager-to-be in Al Lopez, catching the slow, hot, second-division afternoons for Robinson in Brooklyn, the Deacon and Casey in Boston, and, in the forties, Frankie Frisch in Pittsburgh. He learned his lessons well.

Midseason 1933 inaugurated the All-Star Game, this one made memorable by Babe Ruth's homer, which gave the American League's Connie Mack a final victory over his ancient rival, John McGraw.

The Nationals did better in the World Series, the Giants of Terry, Hughie Critz, Ott, and the matchless Carl Hubbell besting Washington without undue exertion.

Hubbell demonstrated his pitching mastery again in the 1934 All-Star Game when he struck out, in order and to everyone's mounting amazement, Ruth, Gehrig, Foxx, Simmons, and Cronin. "King Carl" was a long, tall lefty with a deeply lined face, a quiet demeanor, and trouser legs that extended halfway down his calf. He was famous for his screwball, but like all intelligent pitchers, he flourished on his ability to mix pitches and speeds and to move the ball around in the strike zone. Billy Herman, recalling the past for Donald Honig in *Baseball When the Grass Was Green*, said Hubbell could "throw strikes at midnight."

Thirty-four, however, was not to be a Giant year. Early on, a reporter asked manager Terry, no humorist or friend of the press, for a comment on Brooklyn's lowly Dodgers. "Brooklyn?" said Sweet William. "Are they still in the league?"

It seems they were. The Cards, winning twenty of twenty-five in a magnificent stretch run, caught the Giants at the wire. Tied on the final day of the season, the Cards took a pair from Cincinnati while the Giants lost two at the Polo Grounds to Brooklyn. Justice! That's all Brooklyn ever wanted.

"Me and Paul" won forty-nine for the Cardinals. Dizzy Dean, an original, became the first National Leaguer since Alexander to win thirty. Brother Paul, no character, but for two years a pretty good pitcher, took nineteen. The Cards went on to win a hard-fought Series with the Tigers. The finale will always be remembered for the dust-up at third, when Joe Medwick kicked at Mickey Owen for nicking him as he slid hard into the bag.

Aggressive baseball was the hallmark of this Cardinal team. They would not become "the Gashouse Gang" for another year, but already they were playing gashouse baseball and everyone loved them for it. Although not unique (almost nothing new in baseball ever is), the Gang was audacious, lowbrow, loud-laughing, and successful in a way that was heartening, colorful, and amusing in the wan, pinched days of the Depression. They were mostly products of Rickey's farm system, "the chain gang"—a curious metaphor for courage and optimism in the face of implacable authority and coercion, as was "Cool Hand Luke" in more recent times. In baseball terms the chain gang simply meant total control of a player's career, from the first inning of his first game in Class D, through the ranks, up the ladder, to the last inning of his last game for St. Louis.

To some extent these Cardinals were fortunate. Players for less well organized clubs remember that skimpy scouting staffs, a meager minor league structure, and haphazard training made it difficult—and chancy—for young players to be discovered, signed, and advanced. Not if you played for Branch Rickey. His eye was on the Cardinal. Beginning with a half-interest in the Fort Smith, Arkansas, franchise in 1919, he and owner Sam Breadon bought or gained control of a farflung network that at its peak, shortly before World War II, totaled thirty-two minor league clubs. To stock them the Cardinals ultimately had some six or seven hundred players under contract.

Good as they were, the fledgling Cardinals did not command much in the way of salary. Rickey started them low and kept them low.

The 1934 Cardinals had Jimmy Collins at first, manager Frisch at second, Leo Durocher at short, Pepper Martin fielding grounders off his chest at third. Medwick, up from Houston, Jack Rothrock, a Red Sox castoff by way of Columbus, and Ernie Orsatti were in the outfield. Bill DeLancey, a find, and hard-hitting Spud Davis did the catching. Helping the Deans were "Wild Bill" Hallahan, Tex Carleton, Bill Walker, and Pop Haines. Haines had been with the club since 1919. Frisch ("It sounds like something frying," said a reporter on first hearing the name) had come in a big trade for Hornsby after the 1926 season. Durocher was acquired from Cincinnati, Walker from the Giants, and Davis from the Phils. Everyone else was home grown.

They played rowdy ball, got their uniforms dirty, fought umpires, whooped it up in the locker room. They liked horseplay (nailing a buddy's shoes to the floor) and foolish gags (huddling in blankets around a fire in front of the dugout when St. Louis was broiling). They dropped water bombs from hotel windows on road trips. They rampaged around the league for sev-

Oversize metal baseball contains a radio.

eral years—exciting, irrepressible, challenging, good copy, and a good ball team but, except for 1934, not winners until the war, when the character of the club, despite efforts to keep the rowdy Redbird image going, was in fact changing. The Cubs beat them out in 1935 and 1938, the Giants in 1936 and 1937, the Reds in 1939 and 1940.

These were interesting years. As always, there were firsts and lasts. Night baseball came to the majors in 1935. Seventeen-year-old Phil Cavarretta played his initial games at first base for the Cubs. A strong-armed infielder, Bucky Walters, decided to switch to pitching. And Babe Ruth played his last games for the Yankees. His departure was painful. Vainly and illogically, he wanted to manage the Yankees. Ed Barrow wasn't about to dump McCarthy, but the organization could have acknowledged the sunset of Babe's glory and paid tribute to his role in its success. Warmth, unfortunately, has never been a Yankee characteristic, and the great man was allowed to drift into an embarrassing, ill-defined player-coach-gladhander role with the moribund Braves. Even in this alien uniform, however, the Babe performed grandly and went out in style. He smacked an opening-day home run against King Carl in 1935, faltered through a few more games, then hit three tremendous drives, each one mightier than the last, at Forbes Field, a tough park, and called it quits.

In the cyclical nature of baseball, his replacement appeared within a year. Joe DiMaggio, a somber youth who had grace afield, power at bat, and Yankee tradition in his bones, began a sublime career with the Bombers in 1936. In Cleveland, young Bob Feller took the mound with a stride like a farmboy crossing furrows, and started striking out everyone in sight. Fifteen whiffed in his very first game, flailing at a fastball that seemed the equal of Grove's or Johnson's.

The National Baseball Hall of Fame and Museum was established at Cooperstown, New York, thereby institutionalizing the fanciful notion that the game had been invented there by Abner Doubleday, who went to his grave leaving no evidence that the term "baseball" had ever escaped his lips or pen. The Hall of Fame made a good start by electing Cobb, Ruth, Wagner, Mathewson, and Johnson, although—remarkably—not one was a unanimous choice.

Bill Terry, skillfully reconstructing the Giants in his own image, won two pennants but lost two World Series to the inevitable Yankees.

Indeed, the McCarthy Yankees were awesome: infielders Gehrig, Lazzeri, Frank Crosetti, Red Rolfe; DiMag, "Twinkletoes" Selkirk, and Jake Powell in the outfield; the splendid Bill Dickey catching Gomez, Red Ruffing, Monte Pearson, and Bump Hadley. Even Yankee farms were unbeatable. The Newark Bears of 1937 won the International League pennant by twenty-five and a half games with such players as Joe Gordon, Charley Keller, and Spud Chandler. For the first time the plaintive cry, "Break up the Yankees," could be heard in the land.

In Brooklyn, Waite Hoyt was felled by a line drive while pitching in relief for the Dodgers. A fan, leaping to his feet, cried, "Hert's hoit!"

Johnny Vander Meer, a middling left-hander, won immortality by pitching consecutive no-hitters. Gabby Hartnett, the elderly catcher manag-

ing the Cubs, won a pennant with a notable home run in the gloaming. No matter. The Cubs were slaughtered by the Bronx Bombers in the Series.

Lou Gehrig reached the limit of his endurance in 1939 and sat down after playing 2,130 consecutive games, not yet knowing that he was in the grip of a fatal illness. It is true, as has often been said, that Gehrig played in Ruth's shadow but only in terms of personal flamboyance. Lou's many contributions to the Yankee cause were well recognized and much admired. He was one of the leading run producers of all time: 1,991 RBIs. Only Ruth and Aaron had more. His 493 home runs were considerable and not even Ruth ever matched his four homers in one game and his twenty-three grand slammers. The Yankees have never found his like again. Babe Dahlgren took his place at first base.

This was Ted Williams's rookie year with the Red Sox, Early Wynn's with Washington. Dixie Walker found a home in Brooklyn, where he became "the People's Cherce."

World War II was well underway in Europe as the 1941 season began. France had fallen and Nazi Germany and its Axis friends were masters of the continent. But the shock of Pearl Harbor was still in the future and for as long as it took to play a 154-game schedule and a World Series, America lived in isolation. It was Phil Rizzuto's first year with the Yankees, Stan Musial's first with the Cards. Mose Grove, forty-one years old and struggling, eked out his three hundredth win. Johnny Sturm became the Yankees' second first baseman since Gehrig.

Joe DiMaggio, always a miracle of consistency, hit safely in fifty-six consecutive games, erasing Willie Keeler's record of forty-four, which had stood since 1897. It was a breathtaking performance, in the course of which he batted .408. Joe was stopped one day in Cleveland, then connected for sixteen more.

Williams was also in splendid form. He won the All-Star Game with a soul-satisfying, last-of-the-ninth home run, and he was hitting at a pace that gave him a chance to be the American League's first .400 hitter since George Sisler in 1922. He went into the final day of the season at .3995 and coolly rapped out four hits in the first game of a doubleheader with the A's. Then, for good measure, he got two more in the second, finishing at .406.

Next year finally arrived for the Dodgers in 1941. After years in the wilderness, they finally won their first pennant since 1920. It was a well-beloved team, yet in many respects a curious one, a quickly assembled patchwork of trades and acquisitions that happened to mesh admirably. The senior man was Cookie Lavagetto, who had arrived from Pittsburgh only four years before. Then came Dolf Camilli, then Hugh Casey, along with two American League refugees, Whitlow Wyatt and Dixie. Pee Wee Reese and Pete Reiser, two of Brooklyn's most cherished heroes, came up from the minors in 1940. Joe Medwick and Curt Davis were obtained in a midseason trade with St. Louis. Kirby Higbe and Mickey Owen were acquired over the winter and Billy Herman shortly after the 1941 season began. You couldn't cut it much finer than that.

Hig and "Whitelaw" each won twenty-two games. Reiser won the league batting title with a .343 average. Pete, a one-time Cardinal chattel,

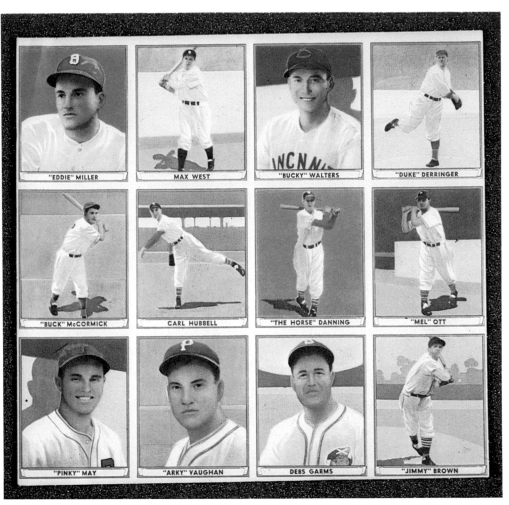

Picture cards (right) *are National Leaguers of late 1930s.* Bottom right and left: *Pinball game and song celebrating manager Cochrane's 1934-35 success with Tigers.* Opposite: *Peerless Charlie Gehringer, left. His star status can be judged by $1 prize if you got his name from 5¢ punchboard,* right.

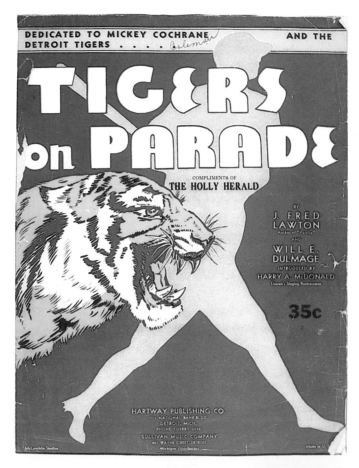

had become available to the Dodgers when Judge Landis, sniffing out some contractual hanky-panky in the boondocks, as he often did, set a number of farm laborers free. (The Yanks got Tommy Henrich when Landis freed him from the Cleveland chain.) Otherwise the Cards might have had an outfield of Musial, Terry Moore, and Reiser!

But the Yankees (yawn) won the Series, taking the crucial fourth game as the Dodgers were about to square matters at two games each. The third strike on Henrich that got away started things off, but there were other chances to get a third out. Brooklyn just couldn't manage it.

Ted Williams won the triple crown in 1942 but it still didn't seem worth a Most Valuable Player award. Joe Gordon beat him out, as DiMag had the year before. Paul Waner racked up his three thousandth hit. Buddy Hassett became the third Yankee first baseman since Gehrig.

To conserve rail transport for military use, spring training in 1943 was limited to an area east of the Mississippi and north of the Ohio River. The White Sox pitched camp at French Lick, Indiana, the Senators at College Park, Maryland, and the Yanks at Asbury Park, New Jersey. Many ballplayers already were in the armed services and more were going in every day. The clubs that made out best were those with a core of veterans over draft age or youngsters with disabilities disqualifying them for service but not for hitting baseballs.

Stan Musial won the first of his seven batting titles. In the Ameri-

can League, Luke Appling, whose fears of physical collapse won him the nickname "Old Aches and Pains," played the fifteenth of his twenty years at shortstop for the White Sox and won his second batting championship on the way to a lifetime average of .310. The Phils changed their name to the Blue Jays and immediately achieved seventh place after five years in the cellar. Nick Etten became the fourth Yankee first baseman since Gehrig.

In 1944 Judge Landis died. He was freely credited with restoring the integrity of the game after the Black Sox mess, and, indeed, by comparison with the mealy-mouthed, self-serving administration of the owners, he wielded the terrible swift sword of justice. For all that, he was a capricious and cranky tyrant who occasionally took the side of the players against manipulative general managers but never questioned or sought to redress the fundamental imbalance of the baseball establishment. Well, he probably never considered that to be his job. He was hired to restore public confidence in baseball and that he did. His position was unassailable. No one dared challenge him and would have been howled down across the country if he had. It was a chastening experience for the owners, who have never given a commissioner such power again.

Strange names—wartime expedients—graced the rosters of depleted teams. Mollie Milosevich briefly played shortstop for the Yankees, Hal Luby the hot corner for the Giants, Oris Hockett the center garden for Cleveland. A 6-4-3 double play for the A's went Ed Busch to Irv Hall to Bill McGhee. Every club managed to hold a few regulars, and fading stars were encouraged to twinkle a while longer. Johnny Niggeling won ten games for the Senators at age forty-one. Mel Harder won a dozen for the Indians at thirty-five. Al Lopez, thirty-six, caught 115 games for Pittsburgh.

The 1944 Cardinals, lucky enough to have such genuine big leaguers as Musial, Ray Sanders, Marty Marion, Whitey Kurowski, Mort and Walker Cooper, and Harry Brecheen, ran away with the National League pennant. In the American League, wonder of wonders, the St. Louis Browns won their only flag since the league was founded. They had come within a game of the Yankees in 1922, in the great days of George Sisler, Baby Doll Jacobson, and Ken Williams, but had never threatened since. Now, by the circumstances of war and a smart bit of managing by Luke Sewell, they staggered across the finish line, one game ahead of Detroit. They lost the Series.

The next year V-E Day came in May, the month when teams traditionally round into form and settle down for the long pull. V-J Day came in the heat of August, the testing time. With perhaps thirty-five games to go, depending on how many postponed games have been piled into late-season doubleheaders, momentum must be maintained and the ill-favored slump avoided if the race is to be won. Diamonds are baked hard, the sun shines mercilessly on winners and losers alike. The American League enjoyed a dogfight: four possible winners and ultimately a margin of just a game and a half between Detroit and second-place Washington. The National League was more strung out, although the Cards stayed close and chased Chicago home.

In August, too, while attention was diverted elsewhere, Branch Rickey, now the Mahatma of Brooklyn, sent scout Clyde Sukeforth to Kansas City to inspect a black baseball player named Robinson.

Below: *The Tigers were the only team to beat the Yanks for the American League pennant from the mid-thirties to the mid-forties. The 1935 club won the Series, too, over Cubs.*
Bottom: *1934 Cardinals (left to right) Dizzy Dean, Leo Durocher, Ernie Orsatti, Bill Delancey, Rip Collins, Joe Medwick, Frank Frisch, mgr., Jack Rothrock, Pepper Martin.*

Detroit Tigers 1935

TOP ROW: DENNY CARROL, BILLY ROGELL, ELON HOGSETT, Bat Boy JOE ROGGIN, TOMMY BRIDGES
2ND. ROW: HEINE SCHUBLE, VIC SORRELL, FRANK RIEBER, JOE SULLIVAN, ALVIN CROWDER, GERALD WALKER
3RD. ROW: CHARLIE GEHRINGER, HUGH SHELLY, MARVIN OWEN, RAY HAYWORTH, SCHOOLBOY ROWE, ELDEN AUKER, H. GREENBERG
4TH. ROW: PETE FOX, JOJO WHITE, CY PERKINS, MICKEY COCHRANE, DEL BAKER, FLEA CLIFTON, GOOSE GOSLIN

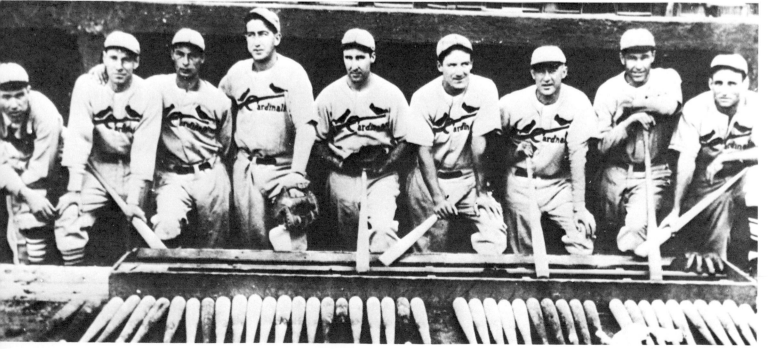

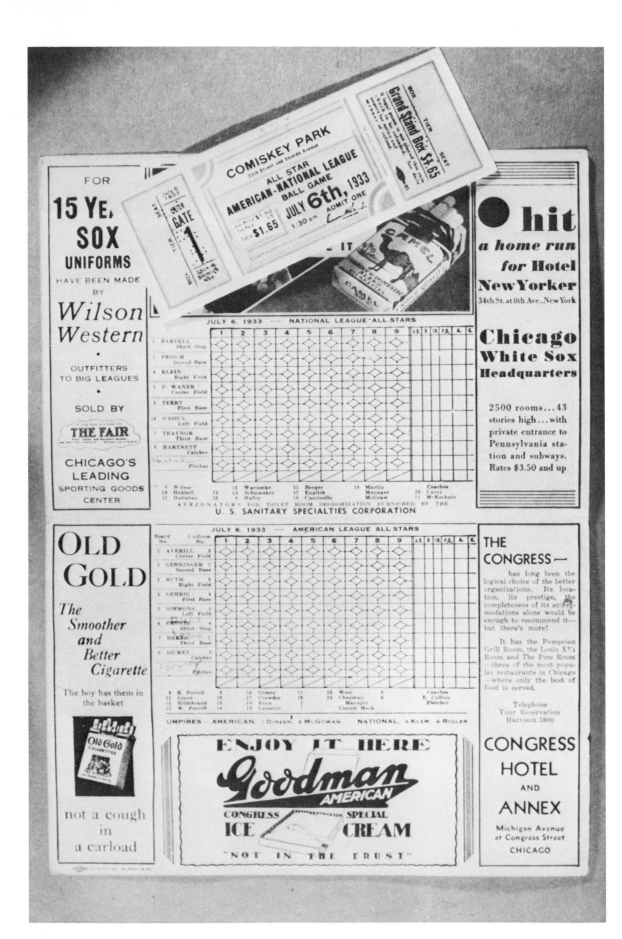

Souvenir Program
ALL STAR GAME

Twenty-five cents

CLEVELAND STADIUM ★ JULY 8, 1935

Fifth Annual
ALL-STAR GAME

AMERICAN LEAGUE
vs
NATIONAL LEAGUE

GRIFFITH STADIUM   WASHINGTON, D.C.

JULY·7·1937

JULY 6TH 1938

NATIONAL LEAGUE
AMERICAN LEAGUE

Official
ALL STAR
Program
25¢

CROSLEY FIELD   CINCINNATI, O.

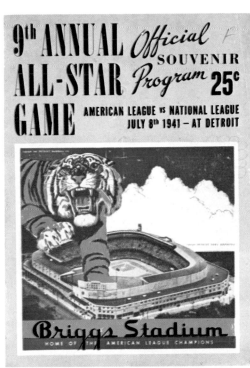

9TH ANNUAL
ALL-STAR
GAME

Official
SOUVENIR
Program 25¢

AMERICAN LEAGUE VS NATIONAL LEAGUE
JULY 8TH 1941 – AT DETROIT

Briggs Stadium
HOME OF THE AMERICAN LEAGUE CHAMPIONS

11TH ANNUAL
ALL-STAR
GAME

AMERICA
vs
NATIONAL
LEAGUE

A

OFFICIAL
SOUVENIR
PROGRAM
25¢

SHIBE PARK
JULY 13TH 1943
PHILADELPHIA

*All-Star Game, inaugurated in 1933, brought
together two truly exceptional squads, managed by old
rivals John McGraw and Connie Mack. Opposite:
Ticket and scorecard. Ruth homer with one aboard
helped Americans win, as they usually did in early
years. Above: Of programs shown, only 1938 was a victory
year for Nationals. In 1941, with Americans
losing, 5-4, in bottom of ninth, Ted Williams hit a
home run with two aboard off Claude Passeau to win game.*

107

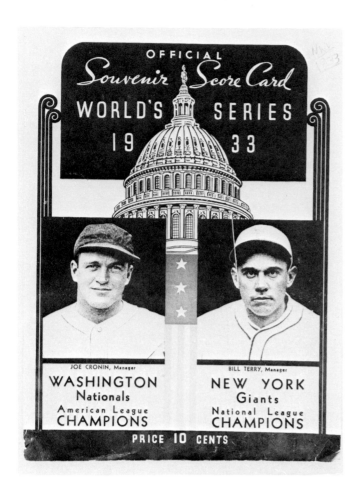

TED LYONS
CHICAGO A. L.

RY B
CHICAGO

PTD. IN U. S. A.

Opposite, clockwise from top left:
*Heroes of Giants' winning
years of 1930s were Bill Terry,
shown on cover of 1933
Series program; Mel Ott, who
smote 511 home runs with curious
batting stance (he kicked leg
as pitcher threw, touched
ground as ball arrived, and
turned his body into it);
and Carl Hubbell, quiet, steady,
brilliant winner of 253 games.
Left: Scorecard of 1934 All-Star
Game, in which he struck
out Ruth, Gehrig, Foxx, Simmons,
and Cronin in a row. Above:
Mid-thirties White Sox
had authentic stars in shortstop
Luke Appling, player-manager
Jimmy Dykes, and superb
Ted Lyons, who accumulated 260
wins for club rarely out of
second division. Zeke
Bonura was in tradition
of big, slow, good-hitting,
nonfielding first basemen.*

109

DIZZY DEAN plows one over

Boys! Girls! . . . Join the Dizzy Dean Winners

Most fascinating player of Depression era was Cardinals' Dizzy Dean. He was funny, exciting, and every bit as good a pitcher as he said he was. *Opposite:* Games, cartoons, pins, clubs attracted kids. *Below right:* Meantime, the Babe, hero of an earlier age, faded away in 1935 in alien uniform of unsuccessful Braves. *Left:* Eleanor's ballad to her shy, handsome husband. *Below:* Yanks swept Cubs as Red Ruffing won two games.

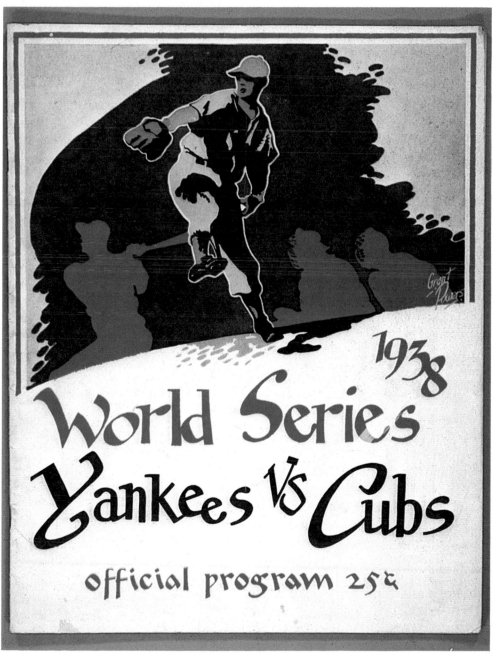

Joe DiMaggio arrived in 1936
to take the Babe's place as Yankee
superstar and inspirational leader.
Left: *In formative years with
hometown San Francisco Seals. Below:
All-out slide scores winning
run in tenth inning of error-filled
fourth game of 1939 Series with
Reds. Recumbent catcher is Ernie
Lombardi. Umpire is old Reds'
third baseman Babe Pinelli.
Opposite: Two young outfielders
at start of spectacular
careers at St. Louis and Boston.
"Stan the Man" Musial,* left, *about to
start his first full season (1942),
would end up with seven batting
crowns and .331 lifetime average.
Ted Williams, "The Splendid
Splinter,"* in 1939, right, *was headed
for six batting titles and .344
lifetime mark, despite loss of five
prime years in military service.*

How to enjoy breakfast!

It's a *"Breakfast of Champions"* for champion hitter Joe Di Maggio

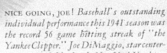

NICE GOING, JOE! *Baseball's outstanding individual performance this 1941 season was the record 56 game hitting streak of "the Yankee Clipper." Joe DiMaggio, star center-fielder for the New York Yankees, began his consecutive game hitting rampage back in May, and kept on hitting at least once in every game until he left all major league records far, far behind.*

As the photograph here shows, Champion Joe likes his Wheaties. He says, "I have been eating Wheaties since 1936, when I first joined the Yankees. I liked the flavor when I first tried them and I think they taste even better now." And Joe goes on to say, "I eat Wheaties four or five times a week the year around."

"Wheaties" and "Breakfast of Champions" are registered trade marks of General Mills, Inc. Copyright 1941, General Mills, Inc.

Tough day tomorrow? Then give yourself this double advantage. Eat a "Breakfast of Champions"—for real enjoyment *and* for valuable nourishment to help you get the day's work done.

Sit down to a bowlful of Wheaties, lots of those toasted whole wheat flakes, with plenty of milk or cream and some fruit—say a juicy peach.

There's flavor for you! A big helping of that famous Wheaties flavor which Joe DiMaggio thinks is "even better now." Flavor so good it has made Wheaties far and away America's favorite whole wheat flakes. (And you can enjoy Wheaties anywhere in the U.S.A.—in restaurants, hotels, dining cars, boats, planes.)

How about nourishment? Well, just try to beat this breakfast combination of three basic, protective foods—milk, fruit, and choice *whole wheat.* Yes,

Wheaties are whole wheat, guaranteed by General Mills to give you *all* the valuable varied nourishment that nature packs into our basic cereal grain. Including vitamin B_1 (Thiamin), vitamin G (Riboflavin), phosphorus and iron. For this reason Wheaties are accepted as a *preferred* wheat cereal by the Council on Foods of the American Medical Association. A *preferred* wheat cereal. That's what you want for your family.

Special Offer! Yours for only a 3c stamp! Family sample package of Wheaties (3 full servings). Also the new Betty Crocker booklet on food selection, vitamins and meal planning, "Thru Highway to Good Nutrition." Offer good only until November 26, 1941. Send 3c stamp today with name and address to Wheaties, Department 810, Minneapolis, Minn.

Stars of game endorsed products in full-color ads in mass-circulation magazines. Joe DiMaggio, opposite, *and Dixie Walker,* left, *were big for Wheaties. Top: Mel Ott was obviously pleased by Velvet pipe tobacco. Above: Young Ted Williams linked his name with Moxie.*

115

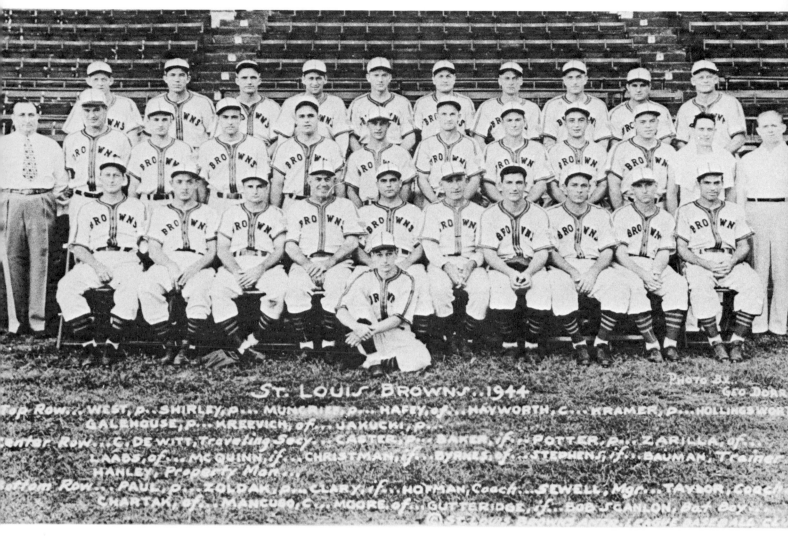

ST. LOUIS BROWNS..1944

Top Row... WEST, P...SHIRLEY, P... MUMGRIEE, P... HAFEY, of...HAYWORTH, C...KRAMER, P...HOLLINGSWORTH, P...GALEHOUSE, P... KREEVICH, of... JAKUCKI, P...

Center Row... C. DE WITT, Traveling Sec'y... CASTER, P...BAKER, if... POTTER, P... ZARILLA, of... LAABS, of... MCQUINN, if... CHRISTMAN, if... BYRNES, of...STEPHENS, if... BAUMAN, Trainer... HANLEY, Property Man...

Bottom Row... PAUL, P... ZOLDAK, P... CLARY, if... HOFFMAN, Coach... SEWELL, Mgr... TAYLOR, Coach... CHARTAK, of... MANCUSO, C... MOORE, of... GUTTERIDGE, if... BOB SCANLON, Bat Boy...

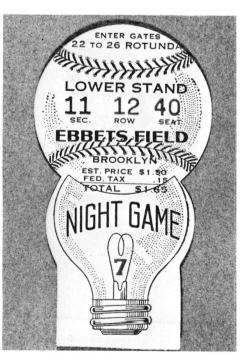

ENTER GATES
22 TO 26 ROTUNDA

LOWER STAND

11 12 40
SEC. ROW SEAT

EBBETS FIELD
BROOKLYN

EST. PRICE $1.50
FED. TAX .15
TOTAL $1.65

NIGHT GAME
7

Opposite top: *Pete Reiser pops a home run against Cards in 1941, his first big year with Dodgers. Catcher is Gus Mancuso, umpire Larry Goetz.* Opposite bottom: *Casey Stengel, manager of Brooklyn in dreary thirties.* Above: *Browns won only pennant of 52-year existence in 1944. Capably managed by old catcher Luke Sewell, they edged Tigers by one game, but lost Series, to Cardinals.* Left: *Night games began in National League (after much nagging by Reds' Larry MacPhail) in 1935.*

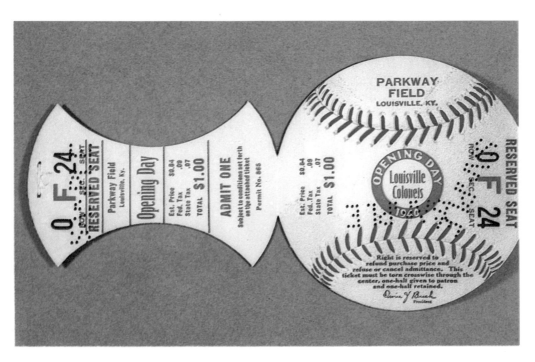

CHICAGO CUBS

1941 PLAYER ROSTER

JIMMY WILSON MGR.

World War II hit the national pastime hard. Many players entered armed forces. Veterans, like Cubs' Jimmy Wilson (left), *kids, and draft-exempts manned major league teams. Minor leagues kept going, too.* Opposite top right: *San Francisco Seals 1943 program cover.* Opposite bottom: *Awkwardness of baseball-shaped ticket outweighed its charm.* Opposite top left: *Pin marks only appearance of St. Louis Browns in World Series.*

Chapter 6

"YOU COULD LOOK IT UP"

1946-1957

Jack Roosevelt Robinson was one of three phenomena that wrought enormous and wonderful changes in baseball in this decade. The others were television and Casey Stengel. There was a tidal logic in their arrival, although once they were on the doorstep many professed surprise and others entrenched hostility. Resistance quickly faded, however, as it must in the face of all inevitabilities. Robinson conquered by the force of example, television by its magic, and Casey by his fool's wisdom.

Jackie was a superb choice to launch the assault on baseball's lifelong racism. He was a natural athlete and an intelligent man, a Rose Bowl halfback from UCLA, playing ball with the topflight Kansas City Monarchs of the Negro League. His talent and character were obvious. What Branch Rickey, bless his devious old soul, could see from the outset was that Robinson burned brightest under pressure, rose highest to a challenge. He would need this quality to survive his ordeal as major league baseball's first black player, to win the favor and friendship of the fans, and to prove, abstractly, the justice of his cause.

Professional black baseball at its best was at least as good as white. Documentation is scanty, for white newspapers paid no more attention to black athletes than did the sports establishment. From accounts in the black press, however, from the confrontations of black and white teams in exhibition games, and from the recollections of the black generation finally accepted into the major leagues, it is clear that there were brilliant players in the thirties and forties, as there are today, and that all baseball was the loser for its fifty years of intransigent discrimination.

Denied a place in the white man's game, blacks went their own way early. The first pro team was organized in 1885, the first league around the turn of the century. The Philadelphia Giants were the first great team, champions of Negro baseball between 1905 and 1907. By the 1910s there were hundreds of independent teams. By the 1920s there was a black National League in the West, an American League in the East, and an annual World Series that attracted crowds of twenty thousand.

Finances were rickety and existence precarious. Only the biggest of big-city teams could play the off-dates in white stadiums. Most simply hit the road in the spring—fifteen or sixteen players jammed into a few automobiles—and played anyone anywhere for as long as the season lasted. This could mean two hundred games or more, sometimes as many as three a day, against other blacks, rural whites, white semipros, and every so often barnstorming major league all-stars. In winter they followed the sun to California, Florida, Cuba, or Mexico.

Salaries were low and uncertain. Josh Gibson, one of nine blacks lately admitted to Cooperstown's Hall of Fame, got top dollar—$1,000 a month—as a prodigious home-run hitter.

They played a high order of baseball. Stories abound of crushing defeats of major leaguers by black teams. Hilldale, from Darby, near Philadelphia, trounced an Athletics team that had Jimmie Foxx, Jimmy Dykes, Joe Boley, and Max Bishop in the lineup. The St. Louis Stars whomped some National Leaguers, 18-3, the victims including Bill Terry, the Waners, Max Carey, Wally Berger, and Bill Walker. Another year the Stars took six of eight

*Indianapolis barn-
storming club,
predominantly but
not solely black,
featured Satch Paige
in baseball act akin
to that of basketball's
Harlem Globetrotters.
Clowns' most famous
alumnus: Henry Aaron.*

from an American League team of Heinie Manush, Al Simmons, Bing Miller, Charlie Gehringer, Red Kress, Wally Schang, and some topflight pitchers: Earl Whitehill, George Uhle, and Willis Hudlin. And the Stars weren't supposed to be as good as the Homestead Grays or the Pittsburgh Crawfords.

The Crawfords of the 1930s are the choice of many as the best black team ever assembled. Buck Leonard, peerless first baseman of the Grays and a Hall of Famer who played against them many times, thinks they were the one Negro club solid enough at every position to have held their own in the major leagues. In their peak years they had Oscar Charleston, "the black Tris Speaker," either in the outfield or at first. James ("Cool Papa") Bell was in center, Judy ("Sweet Juice") Johnson at third. The great Josh Gibson caught and Leroy ("Satchel") Paige was the premier pitcher. At second was Chester Williams, at short Leo Morney. Vic Harris and Jimmie Crutchfield were the other outfielders.

Charleston was perhaps the finest player the Negro Leagues ever produced, although Paige and Gibson were probably better known to whites. Satch was at least forty-two, a veteran of some twenty-two seasons of black baseball and perhaps twenty-five hundred games, when Bill Veeck signed him at Cleveland. Even so, he could still be effective in relief for a few innings at a time. In five seasons he won twenty-three, saved another thirty-two, and lent credibility to the stories that trailed him like incense: how, when the spirit moved him, he would call in his fielders and strike out the side; how he struck out the fearsome Hornsby five times in one game; how he won a thirteen-inning duel with Dizzy Dean, 1-0, striking out seventeen in the bargain. Veeck, who was there, says it was the best-pitched game he ever saw.

Paige savored as well as collected experience and extracted the kernel of its meaning. "Don't look back," he told Richard Donovan, snapping off an aphorism like a fast curve. "Something might be gaining on you."

Gibson, a proficient though not extraordinary receiver, was the supreme black home-run blaster. He was right-handed, with a short yet powerful swing. He is reputed to have hit one out of Yankee Stadium, something no white slugger has managed to do. He walloped eight homers in ten games at Griffith Stadium, one of the tough parks for righties. And he rang up seventy in the season of 1940.

There were many others, legendary names: "Smokey Joe" Williams, a pitcher who defeated Walter Johnson and Grover Alexander; Theodore Trent, who relieved Paige when the great man had completed his chores for the day, and who beat him in mound duels when they were on different teams; Elwood ("Bingo") DeMoss and John Henry ("Pop") Lloyd, the slick keystone combination of the Chicago American Giants. Cool Papa Bell was so fast he could score from second on routine outs. Shortstop Willie Wells of the St. Louis Giants and Newark Eagles, fashioned a unique crossover double play by letting his second baseman field the grounder on the shortstop side of the bag, then taking the toss and firing to first.

Robinson was playing in this kind of company when Rickey signed him, but it was felt he should have an acclimatizing year of white baseball with the Triple A Montreal Royals before attempting the National League.

The season of 1946 was memorable for Leo Durocher's harsh judgment that "Nice guys finish last." A bizarre threat to baseball's monopoly arose south of the border, where multi-millionaire Jorge Pascuel declared his intention to launch a Mexican League glittering with the brightest of American stars. He got the Giants' Danny Gardella and Sal Maglie, not yet the pitcher he would become, and the Cards' Max Lanier, but the top players resisted, despite offers rumored to be astronomical. The venture did not thrive.

Stan Musial and Hal Newhouser had tremendous years. Joe McCarthy, after unaccustomed third- and fourth-place finishes, departed the Yankees, who finished second to the Red Sox. The Series went to the Cards in seven, the decisive run scoring when Country Slaughter, a head-down, go-get-'em, never-give-up ballplayer, hustled home from first on a broken-backed single by Harry Walker.

Robinson had a fine season at Montreal and took over at first base for the Dodgers in 1947. (Second was his best spot, but Eddie Stanky was parked there, whereas Gil Hodges had not yet arrived to anchor first.) From the perspective of more than thirty years the event seems both less and more momentous than it was—less because it is incredible that one man's right to play baseball should have been so important, more because everyone since has learned the difficulty of turning points and the courage it takes to make them happen.

As the season began, the most charitable attitude among ballplayers was stony-faced neutrality. Many of them, particularly but not exclusively Southerners, were antagonistic. There were muttered threats in the dugouts of beanballs and spikings. The abusive epithets, the cruel and peculiar vocabulary of racism, were aired. In May, on their first road trip east, the St. Louis Cardinals threatened a more serious step. Word was that they were resolved not to take the field if the Dodgers played Robinson.

Ford Frick, the National League president and later the commissioner of baseball, was rarely confused with Judge Landis, but in this crisis he did lasting honor to himself and to baseball. "I do not care," he said, "if half the league strikes. Those who do it will encounter quick retribution. All will be suspended and I do not care if it wrecks the National League for five years. This is the United States of America and one citizen has as much right to play as another." There was no strike.

Gradually the ugliness abated. Robinson's refusal to acknowledge it or respond to it, a shrewd psychological ploy urged on him by Rickey, was one major factor. His brilliant and exciting style as a ballplayer was another. He had a stiff, slightly bowlegged gait, like a man suffering charley horses. He held his bat motionless, nearly straight up, and high, his hands at about ear level. He was a line-drive hitter and soon earned the clean-up spot in the Dodger order. On the bases he was a threat. There was no one who could unsettle a pitcher like Jackie. He took daring leads, skittered back and forth, drew throws, faked a run, and then, suddenly, he was off. He had a spraddle-legged run, but he was fast enough and the jump he got generally assured him his stolen base. He never had the numbers, like Maury Wills or Lou Brock, but it may be fair to say that he reawakened interest in the steal as an offensive weapon. Afield, he was intelligent, versatile, and always capable of the big play.

Black baseball, like white, had American and National leagues, whose champs met in a world series. New York Cubans belonged to the National League. Their big star was Martin DiHigo.

123

Brooklyn boy Sandy Koufax came to the Dodgers when they were still in the borough. In his first three years, their last three in Brooklyn, he started 28 games, completed 4. He would do better in Los Angeles.

More importantly, his courage won the respect and admiration of his teammates, not all of whom had been welcoming. There were fine moments, one when Jackie stood alone under a torrent of abuse from enemy dugout and stands, the game almost at a standstill, until Pee Wee Reese walked over from short to put the arm of friendship around his shoulders.

Elsewhere that year, Ted Williams got his second Triple Crown, the Giants smote 221 homers, the most ever by a team, and George McQuinn and Jack Phillips became Yankee first basemen five and six since Gehrig.

In 1948 Eddie Stanky became a Brave. Boston won its first flag since 1914 with what appeared to be a two-man pitching staff: "Spahn and Sain, then pray for rain." Leo Durocher shocked the multitudes in midseason by an unforgivable coat-turning: leaving Brooklyn to manage the Giants. Roy Campanella, the splendid catcher, joined the Dodgers. Larry Doby, in Cleveland, became the first black player in the American League.

In 1949 Charles Dillon Stengel, the peripatetic manager, was plucked from Oakland in the Pacific Coast League to run the Yankees. Fifty-eight and, except for the occasional minor league pennant, a friend of failure, he hardly seemed to be cut to the Yankee pattern or the appropriate successor to Huggins and McCarthy. He was openly derided as a clown, an embarrassment, a second-division fumbler who would preside over a decline in Yankee greatness.

It was Casey's genius that he soon changed everyone's mind about his capabilities without altering anything fundamental in himself. He proved to have a bent for platooning. He moved players about, shuffled batting orders, juggled pitching rotations. And somehow it all seemed eminently sensible, especially since the Yankees won—and won and won.

How did he do it? Ask and Casey answered. Unlike stolid, serious Joe McCarthy, who was always sparing in comment, Casey talked happily and volubly for hours. To the untuned ear, much of what he said was unintelligible, for he had a wholly original syntax. Sentences were disjointed, elliptical, interminable, yet rarely complete. They twisted and turned; they abounded in personal pronouns without antecedents, violated the unities of time, place, and circumstance, alluded casually to obscurities. It was not double-talk, which on examination reveals itself to be meaningless, but a Stengelian shortspeech, a scattering of clues to the flowing thoughts of an agile mind. Decoded, it was occasionally inconsequential; Casey could be as windy as the next man. But it could also be richly rewarding. His experiences as outfielder, coach, or manager for seventeen teams (including all four in New York), eventually covered thirty-nine years and it often seemed that he never forgot a moment of them. "You could look it up," he often said, inviting the audience to check his memory against the record. Mickey Mantle, surveying Ebbets Field for the first time in the 1952 Series, found Casey at his elbow, telling him how to play the angle in the wall in left-center, warning him about the notch in right-center, and noting the route of the afternoon sun. Mantle was astonished. He just couldn't visualize the gnarled old manager as a young sprout like himself, learning about those walls as a Dodger outfielder in 1912. Casey learned and Casey remembered. He was never—to use his own favorite term for a dumb guy—"Ned in the third reader."

He copped the first of ten pennants (in twelve years) and the first of seven Series in his rookie year with the Yanks. Four more followed for an unprecedented five straight world championships. Clown, indeed.

The National League races, often as not, were tremendously exciting and won by last-minute heroics, such as Dick Sisler's tenth-inning home run for the Phils in 1950 and Bobby Thomson's last-licks homer for the Giants in a playoff game in 1951, but the Yankees were unimpressed. Whatever the opposition, they triumphed, usually without even breathing hard.

Their string was broken in 1954, when Al Lopez, a persistent pursuer at both Cleveland and Chicago, led the Indians to a flag. With superlative pitching from Bob Lemon, Early Wynn, and "the Big Bear," Mike Garcia, Cleveland established an American League record of 111 wins in 154 games. Durocher's Giants came in first as Willie Mays got his only batting title (.345) and fielded fantastically. They also had important help from a journeyman outfielder named Dusty Rhodes, who had a remarkable talent for pinch-hit home runs. His hitting was the margin of victory in three games as the Giants swept the Series.

Thereafter Casey began another streak of four pennants in a row.

In the course of the decade, Ted Williams and George Kell, the Tigers' third baseman, tied for the American League batting championship at .343, and Billy Goodman, a Red Socker, won a batting title at .354 while a utility man unable to crack the Boston lineup. Joe McCarthy packed it in at Boston in 1950. The most successful manager in baseball history, he joined a long list of pilots who couldn't make the Sox win, though he came as close as one could in 1948 and 1949. Connie Mack ended his extraordinary career at age eighty-eight, many a long year since he was a tall, thin catcher for the Washington Senators of the National League with a rep for surreptitiously brushing hitters' bats with his glove.

The Yanks' Allie Reynolds, "the Chief," threw two no-hitters one season, Virgil Trucks of Detroit a pair a year later. Bob Feller spun his third. In 1956, the Reds equaled the old Giant record of 221 team homers in one season. Batting helmets became compulsory. In 1957, a New York team made the World Series for the ninth straight year. The Yankees tried Tommy Henrich, Dick Kryhoski, Fenton Mole, Billy Johnson, Joe Collins, Johnny Mize, Don Bollweg, Bill Skowron, Eddie Robinson, Harry Simpson, and, for one game in 1955, Marv Throneberry, as first basemen numbers seven through seventeen since Gehrig. Collins and Skowron, the best of the lot, actually provided some years of continuity, but neither could hit with Lou.

Once the door was open, black and Latino players quickly found places on every big-league roster. Don Newcombe followed Jackie and Campy to Brooklyn. Hank Thompson and Monte Irvin made it with the Giants. Before long there were Mays, Minnie Minoso, Hank Aaron, Ernie Banks, Bobby Avila, Chico Carrasquel, Roberto Clemente, Elston Howard, Luis Aparicio, and Frank Robinson—all legitimate, topflight stars of the game. Robinson, Campanella, Newcombe, and Doby played in the 1949 All-Star Game, the first blacks to do so. By the end of the 1957 season, blacks and Latins had won seven MVPs (Campy three times), eight Rookie of the Year awards, one Cy Young award, and four league batting championships.

Top: *Johnny Podres beating Yanks in 1955 Series finale, for first Brooklyn world championship in eight tries, six against Yankees.* Above: *Henry Aaron came to the Braves in 1954, at age 20. He had 13 homers that year, the only one of his sub-20-homer years in 21 seasons with Braves.*

125

Opposite: *Jackie Robinson memorabilia— calendar (left), kid's bank (right).* Top left: *Button resembled those of political campaigns. Ideal choice as first black player, Robinson had talent, competitive fire, and forebearance in face of bigotry. He succeeded gloriously as player and man, won regard of teammates, fans, and opponents, and paved the way for Roy Campanella, right, Minnie Minoso, top right, and many more black and Latin stars.*

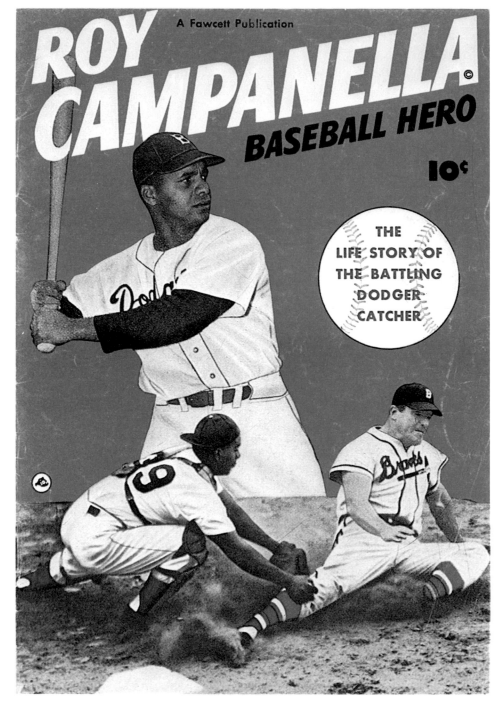

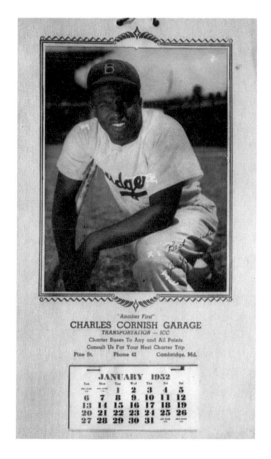

"Another First"
CHARLES CORNISH GARAGE
TRANSPORTATION — ICC
Charter Buses To Any and All Points
Consult Us For Your Next Charter Trip
Pine St.   Phone 42   Cambridge, Md.

JANUARY 1952

Sun	Mon	Tue	Wed	Thu	Fri	Sat
		1	2	3	4	5
6	7	8	9	10	11	12
13	14	15	16	17	18	19
20	21	22	23	24	25	26
27	28	29	30	31		

INSERT DIME HERE
SAVE and WIN with Jackie ROBINSON DAILY DIME REGISTER BANK

The decade saw the end of Jack Robinson's distinctive career. Twenty-eight when he arrived at Brooklyn, he actually played beyond the usual limit of effectiveness. He was the best rookie of 1947, the National League's batting champ and MVP in 1949, and he averaged a strong .311 for ten big-league years. He never let the side down. Most interestingly, once he was past the testing time and accepted as the major leaguer he was, he gave as good as he got and proved to be as fiery and aggressive as anyone. This was just as it should have been. It allowed everyone to regard him less as a symbol and more as a ballplayer and a man.

Television passed through its gargantuan childhood in this period, feeding voraciously on sports. Games suited the tube perfectly. They were performed on a field of action, yet within limits that well-positioned cameras could cover. They filled large chunks of time. And they had numerous natural breaks for the commercials that paid so handsomely. Baseball clubs, the successful as well as the floundering, were avid for a share of the loot and willing to accommodate TV's markets and schedules. Although television did not immediately have the overwhelming power it would eventually exert, it was from the outset a factor in big league baseball's decisions to expand and to scatter itself nationwide.

The alignment of the majors was altered for the first time in half a century in 1953, when the Braves were permitted to leave Boston and open a new store in Milwaukee. Although resident in the Hub since 1876, the

Braves were being consistently outdrawn at the gate by the Red Sox. Milwaukee responded rapturously to its new major league status. Attendance at the first thirteen games at Milwaukee County Stadium topped the entire season's total at Braves Field the previous year. The Browns moved to Baltimore in 1954, the A's to Kansas City in 1955. Suddenly, the majors had three new cities in its circuits and the two-team cities had been reduced to two.

The crucial step, however, was to make baseball truly the national game by a jump to the Pacific Coast. This took artful maneuvering, but Brooklyn's Walter O'Malley was equal to the task. He first gave himself elbow room to move wherever opportunity beckoned by selling Ebbets Field and taking a short lease as tenant. In 1957, in a skillfully orchestrated series of happenings, he bought the Los Angeles Angels franchise and its Wrigley Field, thereby gaining a foothold in Pacific Coast League territory.

In August, as another disappointing season wound down, Horace Stoneham announced that his Giants would be moving to San Francisco, where a new stadium and a warm welcome awaited. New York just wasn't supporting the team, he said, and the figures bore him out. Attendance was down fifty percent from the championship year of 1954. The Polo Grounds (a name derived from the land it stood on, not from chukkers played within its walls) was decrepit. It was a historic park but a crazy one, built like a racetrack—two long straights with rounded ends—which permitted 250-foot home runs down the lines and swallowed up 450-footers in a huge and limitless center field, as Vic Wertz learned in 1954 when Willie Mays turned his back and ran a mile to pull in what would have been a sure home run anywhere else in the world. Still, memories wouldn't pay for an overhaul, would they?

Horace's farewell was a shocker. Wouldn't he feel badly, the press asked, about depriving Manhattan youngsters of a chance to root for the Giants? Sure, he said, but I haven't seen any of their fathers around lately.

In October the Dodgers announced their impending move to L.A. They would play at Memorial Coliseum until the magnificent Dodger Stadium was built in Chavez Ravine.

One point remains to be made about this period. The weight of past glories and the honors and devotions paid to the forefathers of the game are occasionally disproportionate and misleading. It should be clear by now that no particular span of years has had all the best of it. The first post-World War II decade produced, or saw the peak performances of, as many great players as any other: Mickey Mantle, Duke Snider, Nellie Fox, Enos Slaughter, Pee Wee Reese, Allie Reynolds, Roy Campanella, Al Kaline, Whitey Ford, Jackie Robinson, Ralph Kiner, Red Schoendienst, Yogi Berra, Billy Pierce, Eddie Mathews, Phil Rizzuto, and others, depending on your favoritisms or prejudices. There were plenty of old heroes who could not match the attainments of these men.

On an even more rarefied level were the superlative Stan Musial, Joe DiMaggio, Ted Williams, Willie Mays, Hank Aaron, Warren Spahn, Robin Roberts, Early Wynn, Bob Feller, and the extraordinary Hoyt Wilhelm, pitcher in more than a thousand games and winner or savior of 370. If you have seen any of them, you have seen the best.

Four legendary stars of Negro leagues who were belatedly elected to Hall of Fame (clockwise from top left): "Cool Papa" Bell, fleet outfielder of St. Louis Stars; Buck Leonard, "the black Lou Gehrig," of Homestead Grays; Satchel Paige, who gave glimpses of early craft while pitching relief for Indians; and Josh Gibson, great home run hitter, when he was with Pittsburgh Crawfords. Black teams regularly trounced barnstorming major leaguers. The best, like Crawfords, might have made it in majors.

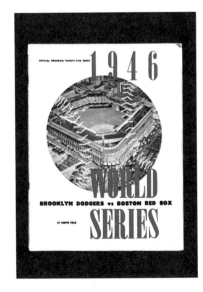

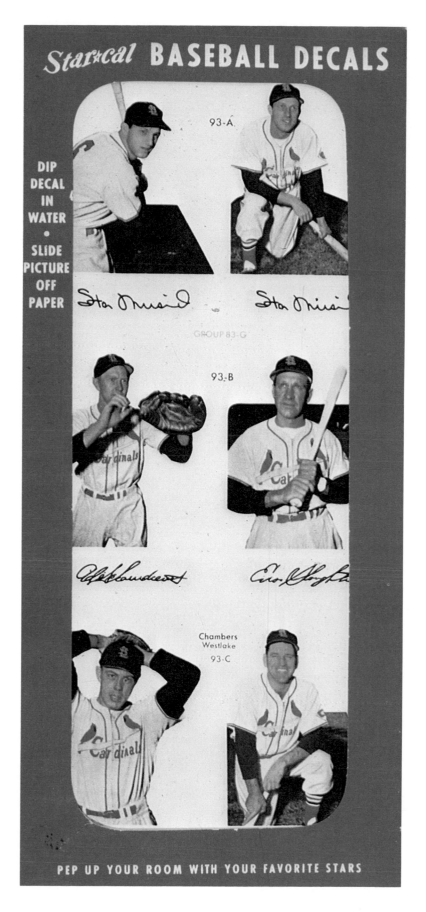

Opposite, clockwise from top: *Thirty-five years after heyday of Grover Alexander, Phillies won 1950 pennant with Robin Roberts, Curt Simmons, Granny Hamner, Richie Ashburn, and terrific relief from Jim Konstanty. Programs for Dodger World Series that never happened. They went into discard when 1946 Cards and Bobby Thomson Giants won. Chesterfield got endorsements of six top baseball men of 1947.* Left: *Decals of Musial, Red Schoendienst, Enos Slaughter, Cliff Chambers, and Wally Westlake, c. 1951.*

Billy Martin

Casey Stengel

John E...

Above: *Brash infielder named Martin and veteran, rolling-stone manager Stengel engage umpire in Oakland in 1948.* Opposite: *Robin Roberts, 286-game winner for Phils, was notable for kind of iron arm seen more frequently in 1890s.* Right: *Well-worn card identified old third baseman Johnny Vergez as Giant scout.*

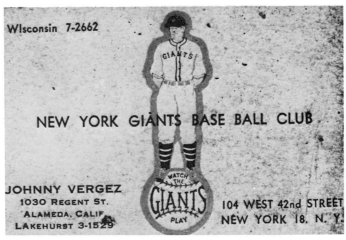

WIsconsin 7-2662

NEW YORK GIANTS BASE BALL CLUB

JOHNNY VERGEZ
1030 REGENT ST.
ALAMEDA, CALIF.
LAKEHURST 3-1529

WATCH
THE
GIANTS
PLAY

104 WEST 42nd STREET
NEW YORK 18. N. Y.

"JOE" DI MAGGIO   "DOM" DI MAGGIO   "VINCE" DI MAGGIO

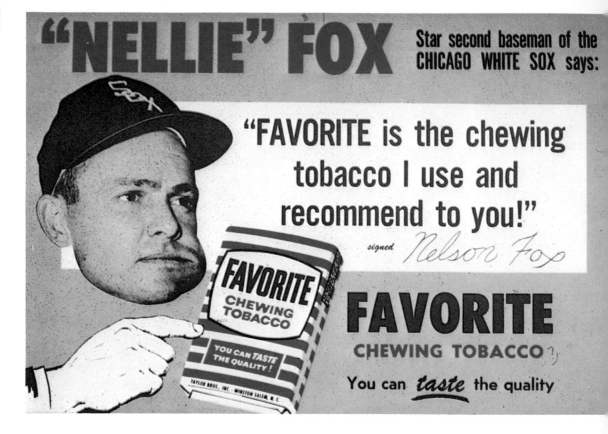

"NELLIE" FOX   Star second baseman of the CHICAGO WHITE SOX says:

"FAVORITE is the chewing tobacco I use and recommend to you!"

signed Nelson Fox

FAVORITE CHEWING TOBACCO

FAVORITE CHEWING TOBACCO

You can *taste* the quality

Opposite top: *Two of the three DiMag brothers played entire careers for AL clubs—Joe for Yanks, Dom for Red Sox. Vince toured the senior circuit: Braves, Reds, Pirates, Phils, Giants in 10 years.* Opposite bottom: *Nellie Fox chawed 14 years for White Sox, 6 alongside Chico Carrasquel* (opposite left), *then eight next to another Latin star, Luis Aparicio.* Below: *Among the few capable players on dismal and diving Cubs of late forties were Sauer, Pafko, and Rush.* Left: *Another perennial loser, the St. Louis Browns, expired, and the franchise moved to Baltimore. Ticket stub is for final Brownie game.*

Top: *Ralph Kiner was
Pittsburgh's premier slugger
for eight years.* Above:
*Willie Mays hits in first game
of 1951 Series. Catcher
is Yogi Berra.* Right:
*Washington plays Red Sox at
Fenway. Senators are at
bat in eighth, leading
8-7. Hits must have been
rattling off that left field
wall. Browns are
on scoreboard, so game could
not be later than 1953.*

Above: *Handsomest cards of modern era were Bowman series of 1953. Left to right from top: Richie Ashburn, Phil Rizzuto, Nellie Fox, Joe Garagiola, Warren Spahn. Middle: Stan Musial, Vic Raschi, Minnie Minoso, three Yanks in dugout—Yogi Berra, Hank Bauer, and Mickey Mantle—Early Wynn. Bottom: Lou Boudreau, Robin Roberts, Billy Martin and Rizzuto, Gil Hodges, Whitey Ford. Opposite top: Cleveland's huge Municipal Stadium replaced old League Park in 1936. Opposite bottom (left and right): Indians went all the way in 1948, missed pennant by a game in 1952, second year under Al Lopez.*

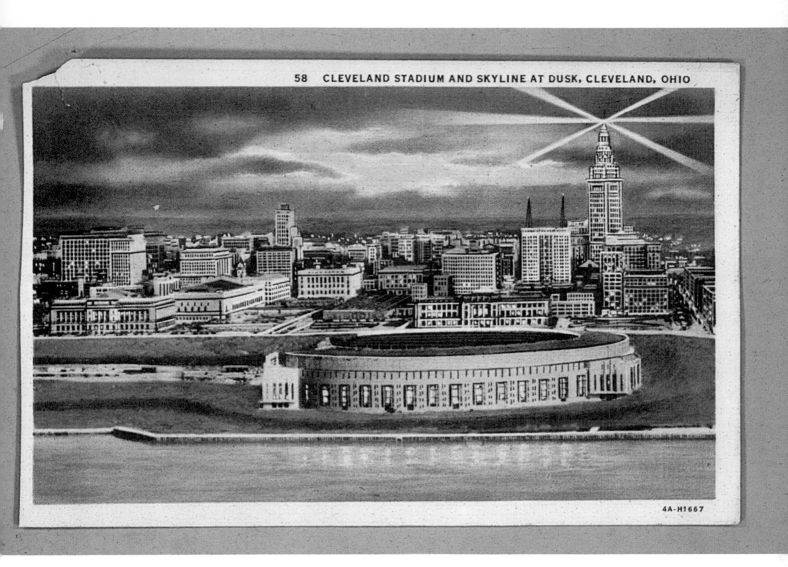

58 CLEVELAND STADIUM AND SKYLINE AT DUSK, CLEVELAND, OHIO

4A-H1667

Right: *Carl Erskine pitches to Gil McDougald in third game of 1953 Series. Fourteen Yanks fanned that day (a record) as Oisk won, 3-2. Campy is catcher; Ed Hurley umpires; Pee Wee is at short.* Below: *Duke Snider home run was not enough to beat Yankees in 1952.* Bottom: *Braves' Red Schoendienst in 1957, first year in Milwaukee and a pennant winner.*

140

BUY TYDOL
FLYING GASOLINE
BEST HEAT
LOW COST
WITH GAS
THE BROO
UNION GAS CO.

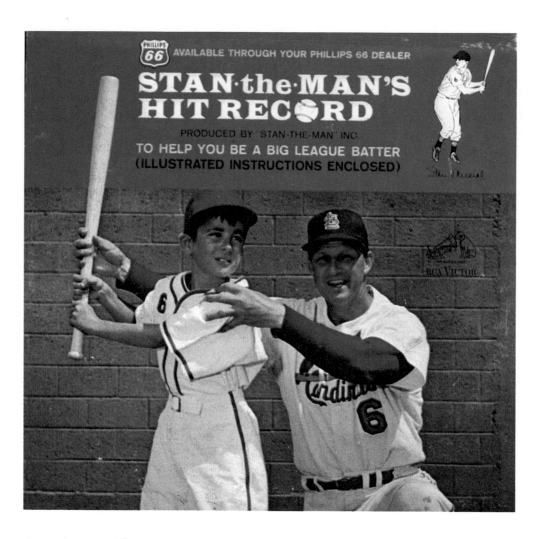

Opposite top: *Plate commemorates Don Larsen's perfect game against Dodgers in 1956.* Top and opposite bottom: *Musial and Mantle cut records.* Right: *Some of the majors' black stars following Robinson.*

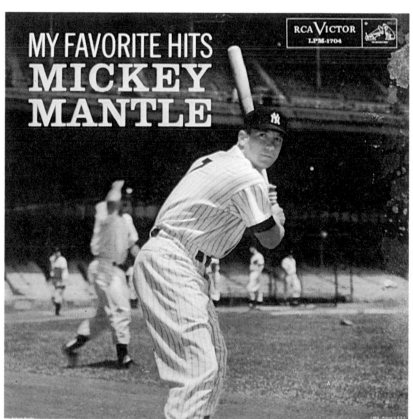

Chapter 7
THE NEAR SIDE OF NOSTALGIA
1958-1969

With the removal of the Giants and Dodgers to California, the dimensions of major league baseball were extended not only in space but in time. Its presumptuous World Championship, so long confined to the northeastern quarter of the United States, and only recently expanded to include the outpost at Kansas City, was now at least national. But because of the time differential between East and West coasts and the majors' commitment to night ball, only rarely would baseball's heartland ever again know the results of all games on the day they were played. It is perhaps parochial, but there was a certain rightness to a universe in which line scores and batteries for eight big-league games were routinely available for the sporting-final edition of the afternoon papers. Late innings of games in faraway St. Louis might have to be inserted at press time—white numerals on little black squares—but you knew that Dazzy Vance had bested Wild Bill Hallahan as soon as father walked in the door with *The Sun* under his arm, and before the long twilight brought a peaceful summer day to an end.

No unfinished business there. No unsettling box scores of Tuesday's game in Thursday's paper—a game completed under lights amid the orange groves of Anaheim when it was 3 A.M. for the sleeping multitude in the high-rise apartments on the sacred turf of the old Polo Grounds.

At first it seemed a profanation to have "Dodgers" and "Giants" attached to Los Angeles and San Francisco. It just didn't feel right, anymore than it would have if the move had been the other way and the San Francisco and L.A. teams had become the New York Seals and the Brooklyn Angels. Wouldn't that have been great?

Well, everyone got used to it. You had to. Baseball encourages sentiment in its fans but has little enough in itself. Milwaukee, Baltimore, even Kansas City, were doing fine. Los Angeles and San Francisco confirmed the trend. Increased attendance, new, free stadiums, and better TV markets justified themselves.

In 1961, the American League increased itself to ten franchises, placing one expansion team in Los Angeles, the Angels, and another in Washington, the Senators, while allowing the old Senators to shift to Minneapolis-St. Paul as the Minnesota Twins. The National League expanded the following year with the Colt 45's in Houston and a new club in New York, the Mets. Question: Why was New York a viable National League franchise four years after a New York team was allowed to escape because it was not?

There was some repackaging and relabeling in 1965: the new stadium at Anaheim converted the Los Angeles Angels to California Angels and completion of the Houston Astrodome changed the Colt 45's to Astros.

In 1966, after twelve seasons of euphoria and progressive disenchantment, the Braves struck their tents in Milwaukee and gypsied down to Atlanta. It doesn't take baseball long to pick up a habit. Two years later the Kansas City Athletics moved to Oakland, and a year after that the void they left behind was filled by the new K.C. Royals. A twelfth American League team, the Pilots, was pitched into Seattle. Wrong address. *Next* year, after a new club's customary finish in last place, and with barely a backward glance, the Pilots moved into recently vacated Milwaukee as the Brewers.

The National League found two cities the American League had

not thought of—Montreal and San Diego—and placed therein the Expos and the Padres. The two twelve-team leagues now split into six-team East and West divisions, which, aside from removing the possibility of anyone finishing twelfth, provided playoffs in addition to the World Series. So you played 162 games to qualify for a best-three-of-five pennant race against a club you had already met twelve times.

The dominant teams of the decade were the new Dodgers, the Cardinals, the Yankees, and the Orioles. The old Dodgers rather shriveled in that Southern California sun. One by one they were replaced by the inexhaustible riches of the Dodger system: Maury Wills, Tommy and Willie Davis, Wes Parker, and Johnny Roseboro. By 1962 or so, the Dodgers were more of a California team than a Brooklyn transplant. Walter Alston, the unflappable pool shark from Darrtown, Ohio, was proving to be an excellent manager and one who never fretted about what the future would bring. In one of the world's more insecure professions, he was content to sign twenty-three one-year contracts with the Dodgers.

In L.A. Alston won pennants and Series in 1959, 1963, and 1965, and lost to Baltimore in 1966. These included the span of big pitching years for Don Drysdale and Sandy Koufax, a couple of overpowering strikeout artists with a combined career total of nearly forty-nine hundred batters fanned. Big D was a top-notch athlete. He could field, he could hit, and he had a wicked sidearm fastball that came very close to batters who crowded the plate, and to some who didn't. He was a bigger winner for more years than Koufax, but he never matched Sandy at his best. That one was a wonder. He spent his first six seasons as a bit player, compiling a meager 36-40 record, primarily because he couldn't control the ball. By 1961, however, he was rounding into form and as the superlative Warren Spahn was fading from the scene, Koufax became the premier left-hander in the National League. He was an extremely efficient pitcher, sparing with walks, stingy with hits, and generous with strikeouts—an average of slightly more than one per inning. Forty of his wins were shutouts, four were no-hitters (the most any pitcher ever threw) and one was a perfect game. Unfortunately, he pitched increasingly with pain, and at thirty-one, at the end of his greatest season, he quit the game.

The Orioles threw off the stigma of their Brownie heritage. If they never acquired the McGravian swagger of the old Orioles, they nonetheless put together some good teams and some good seasons, first under rugged Hank Bauer and then under the low-keyed, highly intelligent Earl Weaver. A winner of five pennants in his first six seasons, Weaver is about the only manager regularly employed who is within shooting distance of Joe McCarthy's all-time career winning percentage. Weaver's most successful combination was coming together in the late sixties and was built around three fine pitchers—Jim Palmer, Dave McNally, and Mike Cuellar—and two Robinsons, Brooks at third and Frank, the ex-Red superstar, in left.

The Cards, winners of the most pennants in the National League since 1926, twelve (the Dodgers, since 1941, have eleven), won in 1964, 1967, and 1968, and took two world championships, including a long-awaited win over the Yankees. Six key men played for all three teams: Julian Javier, Mike

Shannon, Tim McCarver, Curt Flood, Lou Brock, and Bob Gibson. Orlando Cepeda replaced Bill White at first, Dal Maxvill followed Dick Groat at short, Shannon took over third from Ken Boyer, and Roger Maris, traded away by New York, moved into Shannon's spot in right. Steve Carlton and Nelson Briles joined the staff as Curt Simmons and Ray Sadecki left. It was a very solid team, whose ground anchor was the superb Gibson. Unquestionably an all-time great, he is perhaps most memorable for his seven straight World Series wins, including three over the Red Sox in 1967, when he allowed a mere three runs and fourteen hits while striking out twenty-six.

The Yanks continued to fly their own high-altitude jet stream. After winning in 1958, they sank unaccountably to third in 1959 as Al Lopez, runner-up for four years in a row, forged into first with his go-go White Sox. The Yankees regained first in 1960, then lost a seven-game thriller to the Pirates in the Series when Bill Mazeroski, a better man around second than at the plate, changed his image for posterity with a decisive home run off a Ralph Terry fastball.

Afterward, in one of those cold, harsh, sudden Yankee moves, management dismissed Casey and the front-office mastermind, George Weiss, as too aged and enfeebled to guide the team further. Ralph Houk, a strong-minded ex-Army major and ex-Yankee catcher, was appointed to fill both jobs. He promptly reeled off three more pennants and retired to the executive suite, leaving the bench managing to Yogi Berra, the veteran catcher. Yogi won in 1964, which meant a second string of five straight pennants for New York and a total of fourteen in sixteen years. Incredible.

The one-two punch of the Yankees in these years was the interesting combination of Maris and Mickey Mantle. Mickey, the Oklahoma strong boy, was a truly powerful batter, some of whose 536 home runs were among the longest balls ever hit. He achieved some impressive averages as well (.365 in 1957, .353 in 1956) and was a three-time MVP. Yet somehow his career was less than had been hoped for or expected of him. Part of it, of course, was the damaged legs, which increasingly diminished his speed and effectiveness. Part was his unenviable record as the all-time strikeout king and his failure to amass as many ribbies as a slugger of his talents should have had. He ended his eighteen big-league years with a .298 lifetime average.

Roger Maris was an anomaly. An earnest, quiet outfielder of considerable defensive talent, and a slugger of competence but not renown, he proved to be the child of destiny who would break the Babe's record of sixty home runs in one season. It was a tremendous accomplishment that brought him grudging acclaim and no joy.

The year was 1961, his second season with the Yankees, who had acquired him in one of their many trades of that era with Kansas City. Roger began smacking home runs at a good clip. In July he got a pair in each game of a doubleheader. In a hot stretch in August he hit seven in six consecutive games. Inevitably, the countdown began, as it has for every player since 1927 who might threaten the sacred sixty.

Oddly, unlike the seasons when Foxx and Greenberg hit fifty-eight and the fans cheered them on, there was no relish for Maris's performance. Instead, there was bitterness, scorn, even fury; the prospect that Ruth's

Above: *Best fielding third baseman, Brooks Robinson, nabs one of 8,940 career chances. He played most games at his position, made most putouts and assists, accepted most chances, had highest lifetime average— .971. Rated high in popularity, too.* Opposite from top to bottom: *Dodger press pin for first championship year in Los Angeles. Button was no help to Go-Go Sox in Series. Polo Grounds ticket stub for Mets' first home game. (They did not win.) Dodger scorecard cover for year L.A. swept Yanks in Series.*

147

From top: *Buttons mark Braves' first flag in Milwaukee and victory over Yankees in Series, Early Wynn's landmark 300 wins, and another year in career of the Cubs' ever-happy Ernie Banks.*

mark might be broken seemed to be an affront, though to whom was never clear.

Maris, an introspective man lacking in Ruthian exuberance, conducted himself modestly. He was a professional athlete having an obviously splendid season, although the unremitting attention was trying for one of his temperament and impossible to ignore. Under terrible pressure he kept banging out homers at very close to the Ruthian pace.

Part of the pleasure of counting, of course, is knowing that all pursuers collapse in September, the Babe's killer month, when he rapped out his final seventeen. Maris did not buckle. The big thing became whether he could beat Ruth in the same number of games, that is, the 154-game schedule of 1927, rather than the 162 games of 1961. As it happened, he could not. He had fifty-nine after game 154 and took the additional eight to knock out numbers sixty and sixty-one. If he was an unlikely heir to the great Bambino, he deserved better than he got for challenging him.

In this period, Yankee first basemen included Elston Howard, Johnny Blanchard, Kent Hadley, Joe Pepitone, Harry Bright, Buddy Barker, Tony Kubek, Hector Lopez, Mickey Mantle, Andy Kosco, and Bill Robinson. That made twenty-eight in the thirty-odd years since Gehrig. (By the late seventies the number would be past thirty-four.)

Berra, the freshman manager, had the bad judgment to lose to Johnny Keane's Cardinals in the 1964 Series, and in a pretty stroke of Yankee hauteur he was fired and his conqueror hired. Looking down the nose, however, must have distorted the view. Berra was smarter than he seemed and Keane seemed smarter than he was.

Mirabile dictu, it finally happened: the Yankees sank first to sixth and then—cataclysmic year—to tenth. The Class of '66 was the first Yankee club to hit bottom since 1912. Pennants weren't automatic, after all. Houk sought to shore up the collapsing dynasty by returning to the bench, but the dice were cold. The Yankees entered a decade of playing like ordinary mortals. And suddenly New York was no longer a factor in major league pennant races.

The game itself was undergoing marked changes in this period. Primarily, hitting was down, particularly in the American League. The poor quality of the expansion clubs can be blamed for pulling down overall league averages, though not for the drop in individual performances. Only twice in the twelve years between 1958 and 1969 were American League batting titles won with averages over .350. In eight seasons .326 would have been enough, and in 1968, Carl Yastrzemski's .301 was tops. Again and again, one or more of the top five hitters was below .300.

The National League was somewhat more robust, principally because of the continued presence of Roberto Clemente, Hank Aaron, Pete Rose, Matty Alou, and one or two others in the top five. (The American League would pick up a bit when Rod Carew started firing.) For most players .250-.260 was considered a respectable average. For the first time in fifty years regulars could be found at or under .200.

There was plenty of first-class pitching around to account for this: Spahn, Gibson, Juan Marichal, Jim Bunning, Jim Kaat, Koufax, Jim and

Gaylord Perry, Ferguson Jenkins, and Dave McNally, for example. Pitchers' stats were less impressive than in the old days (and no one but Spahn was—or seemed likely to be—in the 300-win class), but this merely meant that long and short relievers were such an established part of the game that aces had fewer chances to score 20 wins a season. Denny McLain's 31 for Detroit in 1968 were a sensation.

From 1963 to 1969 pitchers enjoyed a more generous strike zone. The boundaries in effect since 1950—armpits to top of knees—were increased to top of shoulder and bottom of knees.

Errors also were down, spectacularly so. Leagues were averaging between one and a half and one and three-quarters bobbles per game. The fielding in both leagues was probably the finest ever. In 1964 Baltimore committed only ninety-five errors in a 162-game season—a little more than half an error a game!

Stolen bases were up, astronomically. The 741 steals in both leagues in 1958 had more than doubled to 1,850 by 1969. The renaissance in running was led by Lou Brock and Maury Wills in the National League, Luis Aparicio and Bert Campaneris in the American. Brock has become the leading thief of all time, the others are among the top ten, and Cincinnati's Joe Morgan is right behind.

As is too fresh in most minds to have acquired the luster of legend, the Yankee decline coincided with the phenomenon of the Amazin' Mets. Born in ignominy, yet destined for better things, they were the most beguiling of dramatic heroes: the clowns dignified, the optimists vindicated, the bumblers triumphant, the last—according to prophecy—becoming first.

Baseball had known perennial losers before, most notably the Phils and A's. But there was no spark of joy in their defeats, for interminable as their troubles were, there had been past days of glory, memorable standards of achievement that made their low estate an embarrassment, the players oafish successors to champions.

Not so the Mets. They were, literally, born losers. They were celebrated, even cherished, for their inability to win. In their first year they endured more losses than any team in history, 120. They finished sixty and a half games out of first. "Let's go, Mets!" the fans howled.

Several subtle forces seem to have been at work here. First was the team's extensive repertoire of amusing and improbable ways to lose games. The fly falling among fielders, the bag uncovered, the passed ball that can't be located, the throw to the base behind the runner, the would-be 3-6-3 that pulls the first baseman's foot off the bag, the outfield carom, the infield pebble, the lead wiped out, the rally fallen short, the bunt rolling fair, the home run curving foul—all these and more were in the playbook at the Polo Grounds, and later at Shea.

Second was Casey. There was not much to manage, but he shuffled and juggled as though something were bound to come of it. Still, he was realistic in judging his material and he never tried to look good by making it look worse than it was. They were always "my Amazin's." He merged his identity with the club's, he lent it his class until it found its own, and he put a lifetime of baseball wit and wisdom into tireless promotion of his ludicrous

*Among them, these three sluggers had 1,471
home runs. Mickey Mantle, above, was
a switch hitter whose painful leg problems
were particularly acute when he was batting
lefty. Nonetheless, he hit 536
homers, some of them among the longest
ever seen. Opposite top: Willie Mays is third,
behind Aaron and Ruth with 660, and
unlikely to be overtaken for many years.
Opposite bottom: Roger Maris hit
275—not high on all-time list—but he is
notable for topping Babe's sacred 60 by one.*

LIFETIME RECORD

	Year	Lifetime
AB	537	3004
H	146	902
HR	13	54
RBI	61	310
AV	.272	.300

Bats: Right
Throws: Right
Born: June 7, 1926

BIG LEAGUE HISTORY

Bobby led the American League in batting in 1954. He is a skillful second baseman and an excellent bunter. Came from Baltimore in 1948.

SECOND BASEMAN
CLEVELAND
INDIANS

PULL OUT
HERE FOR
DISPLAY
STAND

Cast in a lifelike likeness in sturdy plastic, this is part of an assortment of many of the starring players in both the American and the National Leagues. Get the entire series. Collect them — trade them — use them as decorations on walls or on shelves.

BIG LEAGUE, Inc.
200 Fifth Ave., New York City

SPIC-SPAN ... the Choice of Your Favorite Braves

Above: *Bobby Avila won batting title with .341 in 1954, Indians' flag-winning year.* Above right: *Warren Spahn won twenty or more nine of his twelve Milwaukee years.* Right: *Minnesota meat packer celebrated arrival of Twins with pictures on porkette packages. Here is big hitter Harmon Killebrew.*

THE TWINS PLAYERS PICTURES CAN ALSO BE FOUND ON THE BACKS OF ALL *Peters* PORKETTE PACKAGES

18 (COLLECT ALL 26)   MINN

HARMON
"Killer"
KILLEBREW

TWINS

enterprise. He played "the Old Perfesser" to the hilt and he survived four straight tenth-place finishes with style and assurance.

Third was the contrast with the chillingly perfect Yankees. Win-win-win. Big deal. If the Yankees were best at being first, the Mets were best at being last. Down deep, it wasn't as good as winning, but for all the unreconstructed National League fans who finally had a New York club to root for, there was a perverse pride in supporting these champion losers. Met fans turned out in truly amazin' numbers, especially when the prodigal Giants and Dodgers came to town. The hope of winning was always more acute at these times, though just as regularly disappointed. There was nothing for it but to love the Mets for what they were, rather than for what they were supposed to be.

Eventually, by skill and good fortune, things changed. Year by year the good ones came: Ed Kranepool, Ron Swoboda, Cleon Jones, Tug McGraw, Bud Harrelson. Jerry Grote arrived in 1966, Tom Seaver, Jerry Koosman, and Ron Taylor in 1967. Nolan Ryan, Tommy Agee, and Ken Boswell came in 1968. The old Dodger, Gil Hodges, that big, serious, well-loved man, returned to the boroughs to manage.

Suddenly it was 1969 and the Mets weren't funny anymore. A ninth-place team, a 100-to-1 shot, they started to play baseball. A miracle was happening and some two million fans came to watch. As late as August 1 they were nine and one-half games out, but after that they couldn't be stopped. They won thirty-eight of forty-nine and finished eight ahead of the Cubs. They scored three decisive wins over Atlanta in the playoff and whipped a good Baltimore club in the Series. Casey was in retirement now, but he said it best: "They did it fast, but slow."

As is true of all spans of time, the decade saw great players reach the end of their playing days and new ones start their ascent. The exemplary Musial ended twenty-two years with the Cardinals in 1963. Ted Williams finished nineteen with the Red Sox in 1960. Spahn ended nineteen at Boston-Milwaukee in 1963, then hung on for two more with the Mets and Giants, wondering where the fastball had gone.

Already nearly a generation has passed since anyone saw them play. These vivid and remarkable men are taking their places among the other impalpable heroes of the record books, dependent on the loyal and tenacious memories of fans to preserve—and enhance—their bright deeds. Burnishing the memory is a pleasant task, one at which baseball cranks have always proved apt. With little effort the past is evoked, the vision is crowded. Players in uniforms now out of style, with insignia of teams now vanished, perform grandly in parks long since torn down. To relish that long-gone mood and setting, and the people in it, is nostalgia.

By 1969 we are on nostalgia's near side. Henry Aaron, playing now in Atlanta, has 554 career home runs. Willie Mays has reached the 600 plateau, but time is running out for him. The many records with which Stan the Man retired are endangered every time Hammering Henry comes to bat. A new generation is on the scene: Carew, Seaver, Pete Rose, Johnny Bench, Don Sutton, and Reggie Jackson. Who will surpass them? Who comes next?

MORRIE WILLS—Infielder

Maury Wills in early days at Seattle. When he got to L.A., they learned how to spell his name.

Donald Drysdale Dean Chance

For six seasons Sandy Koufax, below, *was one of baseball's great pitchers, a strikeout artist with low ERAs and a .732 winning percentage. On same high-powered Dodger staff was fireballing Don Drysdale,* opposite top (left) *with Angel counterpart Dean Chance. Angels shared Dodgers' Chavez Ravine until 1966, when they opened new stadium in Anaheim* (ticket opposite left). Opposite bottom: *Tickets printed by Phils in 1964 for Series that never was. Mauch's club led by 6½ with 12 to play, then, in swoon of the decade, lost 10 straight and finished 1 back.*

Opposite: *Superlative
Hank Aaron, first
in homers and RBIs,
second in hits.* Left,
top to bottom: *Tigers'
Denny McLain winning
sixth game of 1968
Series with Cards.
He had 31-6 record in
regular season. Boston's
Carl Yastrzemski
singles in losing 1967
Series with Cards.
Tim McCarver is catcher.
Orioles' Moe Drabowsky
in 1966 Series against
Dodgers fanned six
hitters in row, tying
record, as Baltimore
upset L.A. in sweep.*
Overleaf: *Old and
new—Bob Gibson,
perhaps the best
pitcher in Cardinal
history, pitches out
of a background of
ballplayers from the
Age of McGraw. The
game goes on.*

NEW YORK

WHEAT, BROOKLYN

CUBS

STEINFELDT, CHICAGO NAT'L

PITTSBUR

GIBSON, PITTSBURG

ELER, N. Y. AMER.

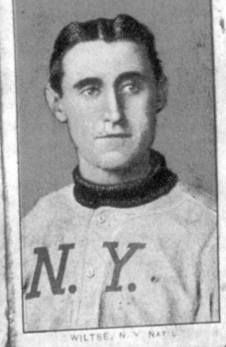

N. Y.

B

POWELL, ST. LOUIS AMER

WILTSE, N. Y. NAT'L

LENNOX, BROOKLYN

ELBERFELD, WASHING

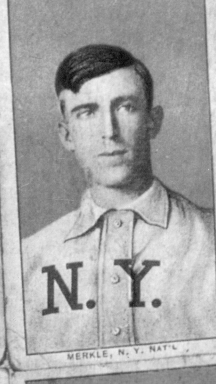

CHICAGO

N. Y.

NEW YORK

DOUGHERTY, CHICAGO AMER.

MERKLE, N. Y. NAT'L

LAKE, N. Y. AMER.

SWEENEY, N. Y

Acknowledgments

The author and publisher are most grateful to Pat Quinn, who served as guide to the collections of baseball memorabilia represented in this book. Grateful thanks are due as well to the collectors who shared their valuable and fragile materials so generously with us:

Charles ("Buck") Barker, St. Louis, MO
Ed Budnick, St. Clair Shores, MI
Dick Dobbins, Alamo, CA
Barry Halper, Livingston, NJ
Donald Steinbach, Chicago, IL

in addition to Pat Quinn himself.

As always, Peter Clark, curator of the National Baseball Museum and Hall of Fame, at Cooperstown, NY, and his staff were fast and friendly in solving research problems.

"Bugs" Baer quote on page 53 is from *Baseball Wit and Wisdom* by Frank Graham and Dick Hyman, © 1962 by David McKay, Inc., and reprinted by permission of the David McKay Company, Inc.

Photographs from:

Charles ("Buck") Barker: 20 bottom, 26 (both), 31 bottom, 41 top, 42 left, 44 bottom left, 48 right, 66 top, 72 bottom, 80 bottom left and right, 102 top, 110 bottom left, 117 top, 126 top right, 130 top, 131, 152 top left and bottom, 154 top
George Brace: 25 bottom, 37
Brown Brothers: 62 (all three)
Ed Budnick: 12, 24 right, 40 bottom, 45 top, 48 top, 51 (both), 63 bottom left, 66 bottom, 70 top, 74 left, 79 bottom left and right, 83 bottom, 86 bottom, 87, 90 right, 91, 99, 102 bottom left, 103 right, 105 top, 107 (all five), 108 top left, 111 bottom left, 114, 115 left and bottom right, 123, 139 top
Dick Dobbins: 18 (both), 19 (both), 27 left, 75 left, 113 top, 118 top right, 132 (both), 153
Barry Halper: 8, 9, 13, 15 top right, 16 left, 23 top, 24 left, 30, 31 top, 32 (both), 35 bottom, 36, 38 bottom, 42 right, 43 (both), 46 (all three), 47, 49, 54 (all), 55 (all), 59 top, 67, 71 (both), 74-75, 76 right, 78 (both), 79 top, 80 top, 86 top left, 90-91, 94, 95, 102 bottom right, 109 top, 130 bottom left, middle, right, 138
Fred Kaplan: 147, 159
National Baseball Hall of Fame and Museum: 22 bottom, 25 top, 40 top, 41 bottom, 50, 57, 63 bottom right, 109 bottom, 129 top and bottom left, top right, 142 bottom, 154 bottom three, 158-59.
Ken Regan: 150, 151 (both), 155
The Sporting News: 84, 92 left, 108 top right
The Sports Collectors Store, Chicago, and the collections of its proprietors, Pat Quinn and Donald Steinbach: 11, 15 top left, 16 right, 20 top, 22 top, 23 bottom, 27 top and bottom right, 33, 34 (all three), 35 top, 38 top, 39 (all three), 45 bottom, 48 left, 53, 56 (both), 58 (both), 59 bottom, 63 top, 70 bottom, 74 right, 75 right, 82, 83 top, 85 bottom, 86 top right, 90 left, 106, 110 top left, right, 111 top left, right, 115 right, 117 bottom, 118 top left and bottom, 119, 122, 126 bottom, top left, 127 (both), 134 (all three), 135 (both), 139 bottom left, right, 142 top, 143 (both), 146 (all four), 148 (all three), 152 top right, 154 left
United Press International: 15 bottom, 17, 21, 44 top, bottom right, 60 bottom, 61, 72 top, 76 left, 77 (all three), 81, 85 top, 88 (all three), 89 (both), 92 right, 93, 103 left, 105 bottom, 108 bottom, 112 both, 116 both, 124, 125 (both), 129 bottom right, 133, 136 (both), 136-37, 140 top and bottom, 140-41, 156, 157 (all three)
Wide World: 60 top, 113 bottom
"Flipbook" photos of Babe Ruth from collection of Barry Halper. Photographs from Barker collection taken by Steve Goldstein, St. Louis; from Budnick collection by Kathleen M. Morehead, Berkley, Michigan; from Dobbins collection by Michael Zagaris, San Francisco; from the Sports Collectors Store by Allen Carr, Evanston, Illinois. Photographs from Halper collection taken by Melchior DiGiacomo, except those on pages 8, 9, 13, 15, 36, 73, 94, 138, taken by Allan Mogel.